Lamyā' al Farūqi

Women
Muslim Society
and Islam

American Trust Publications

American Trust Publications
2622 East Main Street
Plainfield, Indiana 46168–2703

Copyright © 1988 by American Trust Publications

Reprinted 1991, 1994

Library of Congress Catalog Card No. 87-051271

ISBN 0-89259-068-8

Printed in the United States of America

Acknowledgment

The present compilation of Professor Lois Lamyā' al Farūqi's writings is based on the material published in *Islam and the Modern Age*, vol. III, no. 2 (May 1972); *Journal of Comparative Family Studies*, vol. IX, no. 1 (Spring 1978); *Al-Tawhīd*, vol. I, no. 4; and *Journal of Ecumenical Studies*, vol. 22, no. 1 (Winter 1985). We are grateful to these journals for allowing us to reproduce Lamyā' al Farūqi's articles for our publication. The American Trust Publications, however, is responsible for its own edited version.

We are also thankful to the Muslim Students' Association of the United States and Canada, especially Sr. Fātimah 'Ali and Ghulām Nabi Fav (MSA's president) for their enthusiastic endorsement of and support to this project.

Publishers

Contents

Preface

This collection of essays, though written on different occasions, primarly deals with a single issue – that of women. Generally, when we talk about the women in Islam, it seldom goes beyond a few cliche that neither does justice to women nor to Islam. Worse, the attitude is either chauvinistic or downright condescending.

Professor Lois Lamyā' al Farūqi not only brings scholarship to the subject but also adds a feminine touch to it. The combination serves her subject well. With a probing mind, she follows the women issue within the Islamic framework – neither apologetic nor polemic, neither rigid nor flexible; just proper – the hallmark of a genuine Islamic scholarship.

For the Muslim Students' Association, particularly the Temple University, Philadelphia, she was not only a teacher and a patron but a motherly figure. And we miss her very much.

Ghulām Nabi Fai
President, Muslim Students' Association
Dhul Hijja 1407, August 1987

Introduction

There can be no doubt that the essence of Islamic civilization is Islam; or that the essence of Islam is *tawhīd*, the act of affirming Allah to be the One, absolute, transcendent Creator, Lord and Master of all that is.

These two fundamental premises are self-evident. They have never been doubted by those who belonged to this civilization or participated in it. And only very recently have missionaries, Orientalists, and other interpreters of Islam subjected them to doubt. Whatever their level of education, Muslims are apodictically certain that Islamic civilization does have an essence, that this essence is knowable and capable of analysis or description, that it is *tawhīd*.[1]

Tawhīd is that which gives Islamic civilization its identity, which binds all its constituents together and thus makes of them an integral, organic body which we call civilization. In binding disparate elements together, the essence of civilization – in this case, *tawhīd* – impresses them with its own mold. It recasts them so as to harmonize with and mutually support other elements. Without necessarily changing their natures, the essence transforms the elements making up a civilization, giving them their new character as constitutive of that civilization. The range of transformation may vary from slight to radical, depending on how relevant the essence is to the different elements and their functions. This relevance stood out prominently in the minds of Muslim observers of the phenomena of civilization. That is why they took *tawhīd* as title to their most important works, and they pressed all subjects under its aegis. They regarded *tawhīd* as the most fundamental principle which includes or determines all other principles; and they found in it the fountainhead, the primeval source determining all phenomena of Islamic civilization.

Traditionally and simply expressed, *tawhīd* is the conviction and witnessing that "there is no God but God." This negative statement, brief to the utmost limits of brevity, carries the greatest and richest meanings in the whole of Islam. Sometimes, a whole culture, a whole civilization, or a whole history lies compressed in one sentence. This certainly is the case of the *kalimah* (pronouncement) or *shahādah* (witnessing) of Islam. All the diversity, wealth and history, culture and learning, wisdom and civilization of Islam is compressed in this shortest of sentences *"Lā ilaha illā Allah."*

Tawhīd as Worldview

Tawhīd is a general view of reality, of truth, of the world, of space and time, of human history. As such it comprehends the following principles:

Duality

Reality is of two generic kinds, God and non-God; Creator and creature. The first order has but one member, Allah the Absolute and Almighty. He alone is God, eternal, Creator, transcendent. Nothing is like unto Him; He remains forever absolutely unique and devoid of partners or associates. The second is the order of space-time, of experience, of creation. It includes all creatures, the world of things, plants and animals, humans, jinn and angels, heaven and earth, paradise and hell, and all their becoming since they came into being. The two orders of Creator; and creation are utterly and absolutely disparate as far as their being, or ontology, as well as their existence and careers are concerned. It is forever impossible that the one be united with, fused, con-fused or diffused into the other. Neither can the Creator be ontologically transformed so as to become the creature, nor can the creature transcend and transfigure itself so as to become in any way or sense the Creator.[2]

Ideationality

The relation between the two orders of reality is ideational in nature. Its point of reference in man is the faculty of understanding includes all the gnoseological functions of memory, imagination, reasoning, observation, intuition, apprehension, and so on. All humans are endowed with understanding. Their endowment is strong enough to understand the wil of God in either or both of the following ways: when that will is expressed in words, directly by God to man, and when the divine will is deducible through observation of creation.[3]

Capacity of Man and Malleability of Nature

Since everything was created for a purpose – the totality of being no less so – the realization of that purpose must be possible in space and time.[8] Otherwise, there is no escape from cynicism. Creation itself and the processes of space and time would lose their meaning and significance. Without this possibility, *taklīf*, or moral obligation, falls to the ground; and with its fall, either God's purposiveness or His might is destroyed. Realization of the absolute, namely, the divine raison d'être of creation, must be possible in history, ;that is, within the process of time between creation and the Day of Judgment. As subject of moral action, man must therefore be capable of changing himself, his fellows or society, nature or his environment, so as to actualize the divine pattern, or commandment, in himself as well as in them.[9] As object of moral action, man as well as his fellows and environment must all be capable of receiving the efficacious action of man, the subject. This capacity is the converse of man's moral capacity for action as subject. Without it, man's; capacity for moral action would be impossible and the purposive nature of the universe would collapse. Again, there would be no recourse from cynicism. For creation to have a purpose – and this is a necessary assumption if God is God and His work is not a meaningless *travil de singe* – creation must be malleable, transformable, capable of changing its substance, structure, conditions, and relations so as to embody or concretize the human pattern or purpose. This is true of all creation, including man's physical, psychic, and spiritual nature. All creation is capable of realization of the ought-to-be, the will or pattern of God, the absolute in this space and in this time.[10]

Responsibility and Judgment

If man stands under the obligation to change himself, his society, and his environment so as to conform with the divine pattern, and is capable of doing so, and if all that is object of his action is malleable and capable of receiving his action and embodying its purpose, then it follows with necessity that he is responsible. Moral obligaiton is impossible without responsibility or reckoning. Unless man is responsible, and unless he is accountable for his deeds, cynicism becomes once more inevitable. Judgment, or the consummation of responsibility, is the necessary condition of moral obligation, of moral imperativeness. It flows from the very nature of "normative-ness."[11] It is immaterial whether reckoning takes place in space-time or at the end of it or both, but it must take place. To obey God, that is, to realize His commandments and actualize His pattern, is to achieve *falāh* or success, happiness, and ease. Not to do so, to disobey Him, is to incur punishment, suffering, unhappiness, and the agonies of failure.

Teleology

The nature of the cosmos is teleological, that is, purposive, serving a purpose of its Creator, and doing so out of design. The world has not been created in vain, or in sport.[4] It is not the work of chance, a happenstance. It was created in perfect condition. Everything that exists does so in a measure proper to it and fulfills a certain universal purpose.[5] The world is indeed a "cosmos," an orderly creation, not a "chaos." In it, the will of the Creator is always realized. His patterns are fulfilled with the necessity of natural law. For they are innate in the very nature of things. No creature other than man, acts or exists in a way other than what the Creator has ordained for it.[6] Man is the only creature in which the will of God is actualized not necessarily, but with man's own personal consent. The physical and psychic functions of man are integral to nature, and as such they obey the laws pertinent to them with the same necessity as all other creatures. But the spiritual functions, namely, understanding and moral action, fall outside the realm of determined nature. They depend upon their subject and follow his determination. Actualization of the divine will by them is of a qualitatively different value than necessary actualization by other creatures. Necessary fulfillment applies only to elemental or utilitarian values; free fulfillment applies to the moral. However, the moral purposes of God, His commandments to man, do have a base in the physical world, and hence there is a utilitarian aspect to them. But this is not what gives them their distinctive quality, that of being moral. It is precisely the commandments' aspect of being fulfillable in freedom, that is, with the possibility of being violated, that provides the special dignity we ascribe to things "moral."[7]

Isma'īl al Farūqi

Notes

[1]See my refutation of the Orientalists who raise doubt that Islam has an essence

or that it is known or knowable, in "The Essence of Religious Experience in Islām," *Numen*, 20 (1973), pp. 186-201.

[2]In this regard, *tawhīd* distinguishes itself from Sufism and some sects of Hinduism, where the reality of the world is dissolved into God, and God becomes the only reality, the only existent. In this view, nothing really exists except God. Everything is an illusion; and its existence is unreal. *Tawhīd* equally contradicts the ancient Egyptian, Greek, and Taoist views that run in a direction diametrically opposed to that of India. In that view, the Creator's existence is dissolved into that of creation or the world. Whereas Egypt maintained that God is indeed Pharaoh, and the green grass blade rising from earth in the spring, and the Nile River with its water and bed, and the disc of the sun with its warmth and light, Greco-Roman antiquity maintained that God is any aspect of human nature or personality magnified to a degree that places it above nature in one sense but keeps it immanent in nature in another. In either case, the Creator is confused with His creation. Under the influence of its priesthood, Christianity separated itself from *tawhīd* when it claimed that God incarnated Himself in the body of Jesus and asserted that Jesus is God. It is Islam's unique distinction that it emphasized the ultimate duality and absolute disparity of God and the world, of Creator and creature. By its clear and uncompromising stand in this matter of divine transcendence, Islam became the quintessence of the tradition of Semitic prophecy, occupying the golden mean between Eastern (India) exaggerationism, which denies nature, and Western (Greek and Egyptian) exaggerationism, which denies God as other.

[3]This principle points to the absolute ontological separation of God and man, to the impossibility of their union through incarnation, deification or fusion. The principle, however, does not deny the possibility of communication between them. In fact, it is inseparable from prophecy, or the communication by God to man of a commandment which man is expected to obey. Nor does it rule out the possibility of communication through intellect or intuition, as when man observes the creatures, ponders their whither and why, and concludes that they must have a creator, designer, and sustainer Who deserves to be heeded. This is the avenue of ideation or reasoning. In the final analysis, it is this principle of ontic separation of God and the world that distinguishes *tawhīd* from all theories that apotheosize man or humanize God, whether Greek, Roman, Hindu, Buddhist, or Christian.

[4]As the verses 3:191 and 23:116 indicate.

[5]As contained in the verses 7:15; 10:5; 13:9; 15:29; 25:2; 32:9; 38:72; 41:10; 54:49; 65:3; 75:4, 38; 80:19; 82:7; 87:2-3.

[6]Qur'ān 17:77; 33:62; 35:43; 48:23; 65:3.

[7]Any deed that is done "by nature" is *ipso facto* amoral, deserving neither reward nor punishment. Examples are breathing, digestion, or an act of charity or injustice entered into under coercion. It is completely otherwise with the act entered into in freedom, with the possibility of its author doing or not doing it, or doing some other act beside it.

[8]This is attested by the verses that speak of the perfection of God's creation (see notes 4, 5 above), and those that stress man's moral obligation and responsibility. The latter are too numerous to count.

[9]This is the meaning implied in the verses that speak of the subservience of creation to man, namely, 13:2; 14:32-33; 16:12, 14; 22:36-37, 65; 29:61; 31:20, 29; 35:13;

38:18; 39:5; 43:13; 45:11-12.

[10]As the ubiquitous emphases of moral obligation in the Qur'ān indicate.

[11]The verses dealing with the Final Judgment are very numerous, and there is no need to cite them all; some examples: man will not be left alone without reckoning (75:36), but will be brought to account by God (88:26, 4:85).

Chapter I

Women's Rights and the Muslim Women

A ny investigator of the problem of women's rights as it relates
to the religion of Islam, or to the woman of Islam, is confronted by a dilemma. Such investigator cannot help but be
struck by the great diversity in the situations of women's rights revealed in the fourteen centuries of Islamic history – from the
seventh century nomadic and trading society of the Arabian Peninsula out of which this religion sprang, to the contemporary Muslim
communities throughout the world. Yet this diversity does not arise
because of geographic distribution. Whether it is far-off Malaysia or
Indonesia, Pakistan, the Middle East, Africa, or even Europe or
America, similar patterns of diversity are apparent among Muslims.
Recent changes in the national laws of certain Muslim countries
have brought changes involving some regional variations in the interpretation of the Islamic *shari'ah*. Nevertheless, the social structure that Islam created has remained uniquely homogeneous, even
though Muslims are geographically dispersed over the continents of
the world.

As such, it is obvious that any discussion of women's rights among
Muslims must necessarily involve untangling the *historically* diverse responses of these people to this question. In fact, any investigator finds himself facing not one, but four different periods, four
different responses. The investigator must – if his investigation is
to be significant and true – know all four of these phases. First,
there is the seventh-century Arab society in which the religion
grew. The second phase is that of the early centuries of Islam, beginning with the advent of its holy book, the Qur'ān, and the teachings of its Prophet. These were the bases for the Islamic religious,
social, and political movement as it fanned out in all directions from
its Arab homeland. Third, we must investigate the third period of
Islam from the end of those days of early glory, from approximately
the middle of the thirteenth century, until the late nineteenth cen-

tury.¹ Lastly, there is the contemporary period of resurgence from the late nineteenth century to the present day. Unless we know out of what soil Islam grew, the world in which it had to make its way as a new movement, we cannot understand or evaluate its special scriptural and prophetic contribution. Second, unless we know the scriptural and prophetic contributions which guided the members of the faith, we cannot understand their reactions and responses during the early centuries of Islam. Yet knowing these two early phases the situation of women at those times would give a picture which could be accused of irrelevance if the developments during more than six later centuries of Islamic culture were excluded. Therefore, the next phase, that of the centuries of gradual political and social decline in which a third response to the question of women's rights can be discerned, must be treated. Finally, no investigator can neglect the present if he means to acquaint his reader with a meaningful and comprehensive picture of the facts. Many changes are occuring today both in the thinking of the Muslims and in the laws promulgated by countries in which Muslim majorities reside. To describe only the response to the question of women's rights in the past would likewise be limited, and, therefore, an inaccurate approach to the subject.

We shall consider the history of the responses of Islam and the Muslims to the question of women's rights by discovering what each of these four periods practiced or approved in regard to five major categories which are relevelatory of a society's evaluation of the status of its female members. These categories include customs and rules pertaining to (1) Marriage, (2) Divorce, (3) Civil-Political Affairs, (4) Social Affairs, and (5) Religio-Cultic Affairs.

Seventh Century Arabia

Marriage: We can derive many ideas about the status of women if we examine a culture's marriage customs and laws, those which legalize sexual relations, procreation, and promote kinship organizations which suit that culture's religious, political, and economic needs. The Arabs of the northern part of the Arabian Peninsula were, in the seventh century, primarily members of a tribal desert society which was interspersed at intervals by small agricultural or trade communities of settled populations. Even these sedentary members of the society retained many of the customs and ideas of their nomadic forefathers and neighbors. In fact, the Arabs of the settled communities cultivated this retention of desert ideals and customs and ideas. We read of the Makkan families sending their young children to grow up among the members of a friendly tribe in order that they be taught the ways of the desert.[2] In this society of *jahiliyyah*[3] Arabia, two main types of marriage were practiced. One was a marriage based on a very old practice among the Arabs which determined kinship on female descendence. Whether endogamous (that is, between members of the same tribe or *hayy*[5]) or exogamous (that is, between members of two different hayys), this type of marriage was called by W. Robertson Smith *sadiqah* marriages.[6] This name derives from *sidaq*, a gift given at marriage to the wife, in contrast to the *mahr* gift, which originally was given, like a compensatory payment, to the bride's parents or close relatives. *Sadiqah* marriages were of two kinds: One of these was the type called *benna*, a fairly permanent marriage agreement between a man and woman in which the woman remained with her kin. Since she remained a part of her tribe, under its protection and dominance, she retained a good deal of power in her marriage relationship. The second type were called *mut'ah* marriages; these were temporary unions, often between members of different, even hostile groups, in which the husband visited the wife only stealthily and at irregular intervals. In both of these marriages, the agreement was made between the participating pair, without need for or reference to witnesses from either family. They were marriages that could be dissolved by either party and were in general agreed upon for a fixed period of time designated at their outset. The children in both types of *sadiqah* marriage remained heirs and dependents of the wife's tribe or *hayy*. By the seventh century this kinship pattern was becoming more and more rare.

The second main category of marriage was that in which dominance and kinship devolved upon the male side of the union, the *ba'al* marriage or marriage of dominion.[7] Included in this type were (1) those achieved by capture of a woman through war, and (2) those contracted by arrangement with the family of the woman, in which a *mahr* or dowry price was paid to the father or guardian of the bride as compensation for her being taken away from her parental home to live with the kin of the male and for the children to be under the complete control and dependence of their father's kindred group. These marriages were a more or less permanent sort of relationship legalized by a contract, not between the two parties involved, but between the prospective groom and the bride's father or guardian. In these marriages of dominion the woman was the captured or purchased possession of the man, and little better than a slave. Her consent was not necessary, and males alone made the agreement or contract. Minors were offered for marriage by their parents, and there were few if any restrictions on the abuses that this practice might bring. In addition, the men had the right to unlimited polygamy, a custom which was widespread at the time in Byzantium, Persia, Syria, as well as in Arabia. Females who had been unfortunate enough to be captured in war were often deprived even the decency of marriage. Instead they were kept as concubines, a degrading practice which society throughout the Near East of the time did not censure or even frown upon.

Divorce: In pre-Islamic *sadiqah* marriages, those based on female kinship, whether of the *beena* or *mut'ah* form, the woman had the right to instigate dessolution of her marriage. In fact, as we have already noted, the *mut'ah* marriage was not conceived of as anything but a temporary relationship. It, therefore, provided a very insecure social arrangement in which the woman and children no doubt often suffered the insecurities of a one-parent family. In all marriages of male dominance, the man had unlimited power to instigate divorce. The capture-or-purchase nature of these marriage relationships gave man complete power over the woman even after divorce. He was not obliged by custom to provide any compensation for his former wife's future existence, and he could even prevent her from remarrying.

Civil-Political Affairs: In the *sadiqah* marriage, the woman did not become subject to her husband, but remained, like the unmarried girl, the possession and ward of the members of her own tribe, who protected and provided for her and her offspring and sometimes even for the husband who might be adopted by the woman's tribe. In the *ba'al* marriage of tribal Arabia women were the possessions of their husbands. Therefore, regardless of which marriage custom was involved, or if the woman was yet unmarried, she failed to wield much power as an individual in a male-oriented society. In the more advanced settled communities like Makkah she might own property,[8] but for the most part she was completely dependant on the male members of the community. Even in tribes where remnants of female kinship society were evident, she could not inherit – the inheritance was determined through the male side of the family. If she were a slave held, as concubine of her master, either captured in war or purchased she had no hope of even her male children being able to inherit from their father. There was no formal government in that primarily nomadic society; nevertheless, the elected head of the tribe was always a male. The women played little part in political life of the tribe. The two North Arabian queens named on inscriptions of Tiglath-Pileser III are surely exceptional cases, perhaps remains of the influence of old female kinship forms.

Social Affairs: The social position of women in seventh century Arabia, as well as in those lands over which the new Muslims swept in their outpouring from the Peninsula, was certainly unfavorable. Though the *jahiliyyah* poets extol the beauty and virtues of their beloved ones and give glowing accounts of chivalorus deeds and male protection of women, we get the feeling that it is a relationship of domination of the strong over the weak, a matter involving male honor and prowess dominating the female world rather than one of sexual equality. There are numerous early poems involving the capture of women[9] or showing the dependency of women on men and their defenseless submission either to their fathers, their relatives, their husbands, or their captors.[10] Even the insult to a woman, as in the 'Amr ibn Kulthum story, is describes as an insult not to the woman personally but to her status in relation to the males of her family – as daughter of her father, niece of her uncle, wife of her husband, and mother of her son.[11] Although women were usually limited to the tasks of preparing food and making or repairing clothing and tents, they did sometimes become poets[12] and served in the tribal wars as singers and even soldiers.

The inhabitants of some parts of the Arabian Peninsula practiced the custom of female infanticide. Whether for the reason of excessive poverty, or for that of the strong desire for the honor of the tribe – which could be seriously marred by any sexual misdemeanor on the part of its female members – or for the sacrifice to the gods, or as a result of basic rejection of girls in a society where constant warfare decimated the male population and made females because of their reproductive child-rearing duties less suited to the pressing tribal needs, we find that some of these people, particularly two tribes of pre-Islamic Arabia, sometimes buried their baby daughters alive.

Religio-Cultic Affairs: It is difficult to give a picture of the religious position of women of Arabia in the early part of the seventh century, for there was no one religion followed. There were adherents of the various brands of polytheism, monolatry, and embryonic monotheism that were found among the Arabs atthat time. Second, there were Jewish, Christian, and Zoroastrian communities living in the Peninsula as well as in the Arab areas of Greater Syria and in the lands controlled by the Persian and Byzantine Empires. Lastly there were the *hanifs*, who were pious monotheists acclaimed by the Qur'ān as believers in the true religion of Abraham.[13] These precursors of the Muslims were isolated individuals who rejected idolatry. We have very little concrete evidence of women's role in the religious life of North Arabia in the seventh century. We do know, however, that women upon occasion filled the role of priestesses and of diviners among the pre-Islamic Arabs.[14] The *Riddah* (Apostasy) Wars following the death of Muhammad, *sallallahu alehi wasallam*,* were fought against the followers of various local prophets of the Peninsula, one of whom was a woman. But these were isolated circumstances and not rejective of the general rule of male supremacy.

Early Islamic Period

Marriage: Even before the crystallization of the Islamic religion in the seventh century, changes in the tribal kindred groups and in the marriage customs of Arabia were evident. The older maternal kinship ties had become weaker and less frequent. Marriages involving male dominance and kinship were becoming the rule. Even the *mut'ah* marriage, though originally a type of union which gave the woman an important role – at least because she enjoyed the backing and protection of her tribe – had now deteriorated into a means for encouraging males to abuse the sexual privileges involved in such temporary marriages. In addition, the existence of both maternal and paternal systems of lineage and inheritance practices had produced a chaotic system of varying interpretations. There was need for reform.

Islam brought this reform. In order to promote the brotherhood of all men, Islam taught and stressed the importance of the family or extended family as focus of solidarity rather than the tribe which had until that time been such a powerful separating force in human social structure. In fact, it was the tribal forces that were Islam's earliest enemies in its struggle to unite the Arabs and non-Arabs people under a single religious banner. There was a desire to substitute a new bond of universal religious brotherhood for the old introverted tribal bonds. Women, as well as all mankind, had to be assured of their rights by specific restrictions and recommendations in the Qur'ān, in the example of the Prophet Muhammad, and in the crystallization of Islamic law (*shari'ah*) which was accomplished in the second century of the movement. Islam specified that woman was to be a subject, rather than an object in the contract of marriage. This contract was to be a legal, written agreement between two people which necessitated an offer by one party (*'ijab*), a consent (*qabul*) by the second, and witnesses.[15] The two participants were all important in this contract, the *qadi*, or official, was only a registrar.

Islam also specified that there should be no coercion on the part of relatives. If coercion should occur, the woman had the right to appeal to the courts for redress.[16] The wife could dictate marriage terms in the contract, as well as divorce terms. Dowries, one initial and another in case of divorce or dissolution must be written and be of substance. The dowry, or *mahr* as it was called in Islamic times, was given to the wife, not to her family, or her father (4:4).[17] Temporary marriage was categorically disallowed except in the shi'ah sect, and even there it was governed by a written contract and similar regulations.[18] Concubinage was prohibited, whether with free women or slaves (24:33). Polygamy which had been the rule in all the countries of that period and practiced without censure, was restricted by the following Qur'ānic pronouncement:

> Marry women of your choice, two, or three, or four; but if you fear that you shall not be able to deal justly (with them), then only one, that will be more suitable, to prevent you from doing injustice. (4:3)

In many instances, Muslim jurists have considered the clause on the necessity of treating each wife justly (taken to mean physical equity as well as equity in love, affection, and esteem) to practically prohibit polygamy.

Divorce: The innovations regarding divorce brought by Islam were no less revelatory of the rise in status which the new religion was to bring for women. The Qur'ān specifically called for equal rights for women and men in divorce.[19] There is still another passage in the Qur'ān which implies an equality of participation in divorce proceedings:

> If a wife fears cruelty or desertion on her husband's part, there is no blame on them if they arrange an amicable settlement between themselves (4:128).

Divorced women have a right to maintenance "on a reasonable scale" (2:241); and if divorced before consummation, a proper settlement on the woman should be made (2:236-237).

Under Islamic Law there are three forms of marriage dissolution: (1) by death of the spouse; (2) by act of one or both of the parties; and (3) by judicial process. Divorce by the husband or *talaq* was restricted in the Qur'ān by the insistence upon a waiting period of three consecutive months during which time all efforts at reconciliation were to be made (2:228). *Talaq-al-Tawfīd* or "delegated divorce," was a similar type of divorce by pronouncement, but instigated by the wife to whom the husband had delegated his divorce rights. Another type of divorce by act of one or both of the parties is called *khul'*.[20] It emanates from the wife and is agreed to by the husband for a certain consideration, which usually involves repayment of part or all of the *mahr* or dowry. Another type called *mubara'ah* is mutual consent divorce where no exchange is made. Divorce through judicial process can take one of two forms. It is called *li'an* if the court approves divorce because of adultery on the part of either of the spouses.[21] It is called *faskh* (from the root meaning "to annul") or *tafriq* ("separation") when the *qadi* or judge annuls a marriage on application of a wife who has some due cause for divorce like non-maintenance, abuse, desertion, infectious disease, impotence, and so on. *Faskh* divorce is founded on such traditions of the Prophet as "If a woman be prejudicated by a marriage, let it be broken off."[22]

Civil-Political Affairs: The Qur'ān also brought many innovations to the civil and political situation of women. She became a legal entity who could own and manage property herself. Her property remained her own even when she married. She was given the right by the Qur'ān to earn a living and to enjoy the proceeds as an independent individual (4:32). She was included in the Qur'ānic inheritance stipulations, and she had complete power over her share as wife, sister, mother, daughter of the deceased. She was specifically allotted by the Qur'ān half as large a share as her male counterpart (4:11); but when we realize that, unlike the situation in Western society, her husband, her father, her brother, or the next nearest male relative was legally held responsible for her support, we can realize the necessity – as well as the justice – in such a provision.[23] Whereas before Islam, a man could, by making a will, deny to any of his relatives he chose the possibility of inheritating from him, Islam made a fixed, equitable schedule of inheritance compulsory on all Muslims, female as well as male (4:7). Islam provided that a slave who bore the master's child not only gained her freedom – sometimes immediately, sometimes upon the master's death – but also the legitimacy of her children and their right to inherit with equality, as though they were born to a free woman.[24]

Women played an important role in the early centuries of Islam, even acieving power in state affairs. 'A'ishah, one of the wives of the Prophet Muhammad is a case in point. Not only was she very active in the political disturbances following the murder of the third caliph 'Uthmān but in the famous Battle of the Camel in 656, she cheered on and led the troops opposing 'Ali from the back of a camel at the head of the foray. There is also a famous story about a woman who held a heated argument with the caliph 'Umar over the reduction and limitation of dowries. After she rose in the mosque and presented her views, the caliph bowed to the lady in admiration and declared his acceptance of the validity of her case.[25]

Social Affairs: With Islam's blow to tribalism and its move out of the desert environment, new social and cultural ideas regarding women sprang up. The Qur'ān insistence on equality for the sexes, and early Islam's drive for education brought many benefits to women in the early centuries. Women became poets, writers, and leaders in various fields. Sukayanah (d. 735 A.C.), daughter of Husayn ibn 'Ali, was a leader in fashion, beauty, and literature, whose salons and intellectual parties were famous in the entire Muslim World of that time. Rabi'ah al 'Adawiyyah, in the second century of Islam, was one of the most famous Sufi poets. Sufi orders admitted women, who at times became leaders of those religious communities. These women of early Islam were not veiled. They were enjoined by Islam to be proprietous, but they were never told to live lives of segregation and isolation. It is obvious from the following passage that the Qur'ān enjoins on both men and women the same sense of modesty.

> Say to the believing men that they should lower their gaze and guard their modesty: that will make for greater purity for them: and God is well acquainted with all that they do. And say to the believing women that they should lower their gaze and guard their modesty; that they should not display their beauty and ornaments except what (must ordinarily) appear thereof ... (24:30-31).

The Arabic expression "illā mā dhahar" used in this passage for "What (must ordinarily) appear thereof" is one which signifies recommending a conformance with the prevailing customs of a region or period, and says nothing about a necessity for the veil, for all-enveloping wraps that left only the hands exposed, or for the crushing custom of purdah ("screen" or "shield") which cut women off completely from a male-oriented world. Female infanticide was prohibited in strong terms by Prophet Muhammad as well as the Qur'ān. The Qur'ān considered both girl and boy babies as gifts from God to be rejoiced over and nourished to maturity (81:8-9; 16:58-59).

Religio-Cultic Affairs: Islam brought many changes to the status of women. In fact, a noted authority on Islamic law has written that "probably the most important legal reforms introduced by Islam refer to the rights of women."[26] Perhaps none was more determinant of her new position than the Qur'ānic statements guaranteeing her equality with men in religious life. All duties incumbent on the male are also incumbent on the female. The obligations of pilgrimage, zakah (legal alms), fasting, prayer, and so on, all aqually fall on both (33:35). Women are according to the Qur'ān also absolutely equal in final judgment:

> Never will I suffer to be lost the work of any of you, be he male or female: you are member, one of another ... (3:195).

> If any do deeds of righteousness, be they male or female and have faith, they will enter heaven, and not the least injustice will be done to them (4:124).

There was no concept of original sin blamed on women in the religion of Islam. Far from attributing the idea of evil temptress to Eve in her role as the first woman, the Qur'ān put the blame for the mistake in the Garden of Eden on both Adam and his wife (7:20-25; 20:121)). They both repented and asked forgiveness. Also, woman is the mother of all men and her role holds no contemptuous connotations. Likewise, the creation story in the Qur'ān, from which God created the first person and that person's mate, is not designated as male, thereby perhaps giving him prior importance. In fact, because of grammatical requirements (nafs is a feminine word in Arabic as is the word wahidah meaning "one person"), the first person created is treated as feminine. Despite this fact, English translations, influenced by the Old Testament story, make the transfer to masculine when translating the relevant passage from the Qur'ān (4:1).

In conformance with pre-Islamic practice, women could be involved in religious prayer, and they did go regularly to the mosque in the time of the Prophet.[27] The particular nature of Islamic formal communal prayer with its many prostrations and genuflexions made it proper that men form their lines in front and woman form theirs in the back of the prayer chamber. Anyone who knows the Islamic prayer can understand that this is not meant as an indication of inequality.

The Centuries of Decline (1250-1900)

The next period we shall investigate is that following the Mongol invasions and lasting until the late nineteenth century. It is in this long period following the political and physical disasters accompanying those tribal movements of fierce nomads from the East that the picture of woman's role in Islamic society began to deteriorate.

Marriage: It was in this period that women relinquished gradually the rights that the Qur'ān, the *Sunnah* of the Prophet Muhammad,[28] and the early Muslim jurists who interpreted these two prime sources of Islamic law had provided her. Though the marriage was meant to be a contract between the two persons involved, it was during this period of decline, decline not only of women's rights, but of political, social, and economic features as well, that parents and guardians became the determiners and makers of the marriage agreements. Though still retaining a legal right to consent or reject, most girls felt it their filial duty to marry as their relatives chose. Even small children were married to each other, the marriage to be consummated upon the pair's reaching puberty. And though Islamic law provided that any child marriage could be rejected before consummation if either of the participants desired, this was rarely done in this period and might have caused dire trouble with her relatives for a helpless young girl. Though given the right by Islamic law to include in the marriage contract protective stipulations for herself against polygamy and undesired divorce, such rights were not always claimed by the women, uneducated as they were and unaware of those statutes of the *shari'ah* which protected them. Uncontrolled polygamy and concubinage flourished, especially among the rich, despite the Qur'ān's precise legislation.

Divorce: Though there were laws to provide women with means of attaining a divorce under reasonable circumstances, it became the custom for men alone to exercise their rights in this regard. *Talaq* or repudiation divorce became the almost exclusive pattern of divorce, and it was abused in various ways. Though this pronouncement was to be made in a period of *tuhr* ("purity" – that is not during the menstruation period), or, in another form, in three successive periods of *tuhr*, women were sometimes divorced by husbands who did not adhere to these stipulations. Though a three month waiting period (*'iddah*) was required before the divorce became final, men sometimes ignored this chance for reconciliation and severed all ties with their wives immediately and without forewarning. With a triple repudiation "I divorce you, I divorce you, I divorce you!" in a fit of male anger, the wife was irrevocably separated from her husband.[29]

Civil-Political Affairs: Along with the subjugation of women to their husbands or male relatives, we would expect to find little progress in the civil and political rise of women in this period. As women became physically, economically, and socially more dependent, the average education level of girls, which had gone up during the first centuries of Islam, gradually sank lower and lower. And this of course had increasingly adverse effects on the role that women played in life. It become exceptional for her to actually claim her legal rights, whether those were in connection with inheritance, the management of her property, or the fulfilment of her duty as adult member of the community.

Social Affairs: It is in her social role that the degradation of many Muslim women of this period has been most notorious. Everyone has read of the profligate concubinage and polygamy, as well as the veiled prisoners of the harem. Despite the fact that concubinage had been forbidden, that polygamy had been regulated and discouraged, and that the early Muslims had not condoned such customs as the harem, purdah, and the veil, these practices which revealed woman's subordinate role in life have been associated with Islam and Islamic culture by many Muslims as well as non-Muslims who did not bother to know the facts about the religion, who were given misleading information, or who knew only this one period of Islam's history. Though the society did not revert to the horrible pre-Islamic practice of female infanticide, the birth of a girl to any family was considered a misfortune to be mourned, the birth of a boy a blessing to be celebrated. And no wonder! For the lot of the girl was in most cases that of a second class citizen who did not receive an adequate education to prepare her for anything but the role of household servant. Her role as wife and mother was only inadequately filled, for she was not educated sufficiently to care for more than the barest physical needs of her children and husband. It gradually became the rule that women had no function in life beyond the immediate family circle inside the home. Though Islam, realizing the human need for a mother's care, had given women stronger custody rights over children than their fathers,[20] these rights were gradually left unclaimed; and custody, except in unusual cases where the religious courts stepped in to reverse the practice, was automatically given to the male side of the family.

Religio-Cultic Affairs: Though God in the Qur'ān[31] had laid great stress on the equality of the sexes, and in the early period of Islam this spirit had prevailed, later centuries brought reversals in the stature of women in religious affairs as in other matters. As women played less and less important roles in the family and community life, they also played less and less part in the religious life of the community. It became the practice for women to avoid the congregational mosque for their prayer and to remain at home, thus shutting themselves off from the spiritual and educative and community life which had been focussed in the mosques of the early centuries. In fact, one writer from Egypt has estimated that as many as ninety per cent of the veiled women of Egypt not only do not go to the mosque to pray, but they do not pray at all, nor know of the other duties of Islam any more than the names.[32]

What went wrong? What happened that made woman become ashamed of her sex, that made her retire to a position of weakness and subservience to the male in these later centuries of Islam?

Many explanations are possible. Perhaps no one of them is exclusively responsible. We have already mentioned the political disturbances accompanying the tribal movements in Central Asia which spilled over into Islamic lands. Political upheavals as devastating as these Turkish and Mongol invasions were, are bound to produce a shock of widespread effect in the culture. And it was in fact this shock that forced the culture into a period of conservatism which grew steadily stronger as that culture sought to maintain its equilibrium under the impact of the new influences from outside. Feudalism may have been a second cause for the deterioration of women's rights. As the problems of security increased, as the original unity of the Islamic *ummah* or community splintered, as wealth was gradually concentrated in the hands of fewer and fewer people, the Islamic society sank into a feudalistic period from which, in some lands, it did not completely escape up to the present day. A feudal society not only takes advantage of the peasants; but, because of the need for a steady supply of warriors by the petty rulers, because of the law of the jungle which feudalism encourages, and because of the resultant need for protection, the woman became gradually a drag on society which could contribute little and was always in need of protection. A third explanation of the reversal of the rights Islam had won for women is that they were the result of the change which occurs when a tribal society moves to a foreign or urban environment. While a tribal people lives its life among known relatives or friends, there were few dangers to the preservation of the tribe's exclusiveness, its normal kinship patterns, and the control of its members. But as these tribal and country people moved to new lands and to urban areas, this control was endangered and the society instinctively began protecting its women with great care.[33] It was then that the Muslims took on the Persian and Byzantine customs of the face veil and the harem. Women were gradually forced into a more and more secluded and oppressed life. A fourth explanation is that after the weakening of the initial strength of the Islamic movement the basic customs and practices of the areas where Islam had brought its message began to reassert themselves in opposition to the beliefs and principles of the Qur'ānic teaching. For example, among some Berber tribes of North Africa, marriage, following pre-Islamic Berber custom, is still a form of purchase wherein the husband pays the *mahr* or dower to the bride's father and demands it back should the wife be repudiated. Also, though Islam specifically forbids this (4:7), Berber women have sometimes been denied their inheritance rights because the official tribunals applied, through ignorance, a local customary law instead of the *shari'ah.*[34] Whichever of these causes is responsible or whatever other causes combined to produce an unfavorable reversal of the Islamic advance in regard to the status of women, we know that by the late nineteenth century, her situation was in crying need of reform.

Reform Period (1900-1970's)

Then in the late nineteenth century a period of reform began. This was partly due to influences from Europe and America, where the liberalizing influences of the Enlightenment period, as well as the Industrial Revolution with its need for women to be included in the work force, had brought about revolutionay changes in the thinking about women's status, if not always concrete results.[35] It was also due to an awakening from within the Muslim World. Reformers in various countries began advocating a new look at women's rights. The well-known writer and activist Jamal al Din al Afghani[36] and his student Muhammad 'Abduh[37] included reforms in the traetment of women in their movements. Qasim Amin[38] was another active leader in the movement for emancipation of women as viewed from within the Islamic context. While some countries (notably Turkey under Kemal Ataturk) sought to get their inspiration from non-Islamic sources, most of the Islamic World's reformers went back into their own legacy to re-discover the basic tenets and principles which were outlined in the Qur'ān in the seventh century and to reinterpret them in the light of the new situations of the twentieth century. The Qur'ān, after all, had not pretended to be more than a set of principles which must – through the help of *qiyas* (analogical intepretation), knowledge of the hadith literature (that is the example of the Prophet and his companions), *ijma'* (community consensus), and *ijtihad* (independent interpretation by the jurists of the basic principles) be expanded into a body of law which could answer all the problems of the Muslim people in whatever part of the world they lived. Most of these reformers sought change through a reinterpretation of the original sources of the *shari'ah* rather than in a completely new creation based on a foreign cultural heritage. Many women organizations in Pakistan and in Middle East were formed which together with the efforts of individual leaders have helped to bring about changes throughout the Muslim World.

Marriage: Nowhere have these changes been more obvious than in the marriage reforms. Polygamy has been brought under control again, as Prophet Muhammad and Allah the Exalted in the Qur'ān sought to do in the seventh century. Today it is the rare exception. Most countries have put it under judicial regulation and in some countries it has been prohibited altogether[39] on the ground that the Qur'ānic stipulation of absolute equal treatment makes polygamous marriage virtually impossible. Child marriage has been virtually abandoned in the Muslim countries. And marriage without consent has been combated by new laws which reinforce the original Islamic principles for equality.

Divorce: As for divorce, a wife has in almost every Muslim country now the ability to get a divorce if she has reasonable grounds. In addition, in nearly all the Arab countries the *talaq* (repudiation) divorce without arbitration or *'iddah* (waiting period) has been discouraged. In Tunisia, in fact, every divorce must be arranged in a court of law.[40] In Pakistan no divorce is effective until ninety days after being reported to the President of the relevant Union Council in order to provide for arbitration.[41] And in Singapore no divorce can be granted without mutual consent, except through a *shari'ah* court after conciliation has been attempted.[42]

Civil-Political Affairs: In most Muslim countries women have been granted the vote.[43] The right of woman to own and manage her own property after marriage as well as before has been reaffirmed by contemporary laws.[44] Not only as an individual but as a member of women's organizations, the Muslim woman has been increasing her efforts to improve the social and political situation in her homeland. Women's societies for social services and for cooperation with governments in making labor laws and social legislation have been active in many countries. Women's branches of the Red Crescent (counterpart of the Red Cross) work for the benefit of all in times of national catastrophe and need. In revolutions for freedom, whether in Algeria, Egypt, or Pakistan women have been known and respected for their conttribution to the national cause.

Social Affairs: Although the first reformers in the Muslim World were men, in the early twentieth century there were instances of active participation by women as well. Women's magazines and a number of women writers began to appear in various countries. Standards of education for women improved, and complete educations for them are becoming ever more common. The Saudi Arabian government was one of the last to institute women's education.[45] As the number of girls involved in the educational process increases dramatically,[46] new positions open up for them. There are now women who are doctors, lawyers, artists, and teachers and others who take part in the business world. The harem, purdah, and the veil are disappearing from city society. They were never an important part of rural peasant life.

Religio-Cultic Affair: There has been little progress to reintegrate the women of the Muslim World into the religious life of the community except in the new immigrant communities of Canada and the United States.

There has been much progress in other fields, but Muslim women, on the whole, still lag far behind men in their status and their capabilities. As in other parts of the world, including the most "advanced" societies of Europe and America, the lag in the education of girls is one of the major factors for this discrepancy.[47] In the Muslim World the percentages of women getting good education are less favorable and therefore the situation of the Muslim woman is more precarious. Despite Prophet Muhammad's command for the education of every female as well as male,[48] less .than half of the young women in Muslim countries receive more than the most rudimentary education. Until this lack can be corrected, the insight and equipment to be independent will be weak in the Muslim woman, those rights and privileges granted to her by Islam will never be attained, and the fact of their existence will not even be realized.

Islam brought women from the position of chattel in marriage to that of equal partners. In the matter of divorce, she changed from a completely impotent bystander, to one who could initiate divorce proceedings and claim her rights of dowry and inheritance. From a position of legal nonetity, she became a legal personality in the full sense of the term, able to hold property, entitled to a just share of her husband's and family's inheritance property. Socially, with education equally required of her as well as of every man by Islam, she rose to a position of social and cultural influence and service. Even in religio-cultic practices and duties, woman was asked and expected to play a role equal to that of man, insofar as her special physical characteristics and maternal duties allowed. Her position in early

Islam was really an exemplary one, one that should be studied and known by every woman as well as every liberationist in the tweniteth century – in America as well as in the Muslim World. The Muslim woman, if she is true to the principles of her religion, has lessons in equality to teach the Westerner, and her descendants in the East have to learn anew the role demanded of them by their religion. Orientalists and orientals zealous for modernization should cease to put the blame on Islam, a blame which instead deserves to fall on their own ignorance of the faith and on the political and social decline which their nations suffered in the past.

Notes

* Means "upon whom be peace" and is said by the Muslims out of respect and love for their prophet whenever his name is mentioned.

1. When one speaks of periods in the evolution of any culture, it is usually difficult to assign any one precise date as a turning point. We may mark the beginning of the third phase, however, as coinciding roughly with the invasions of the Islamic World by the Mongol tribes around the middle of the thirteenth century, A.C.

2. Ibn Ishaq, *Sirat Rasul Allah*, tr. A. Gullaume, *The Life of Muhammad* (London. Oxford University Press, 1955), pp. 69-73, tells the story of Muhammad's foster parentage and his early years of life in the desert.

3. This is a name given to pre-Islamic Arabia by the Qur'ān and the Muslims. It is derived from the root "jahil" and has been generally thought to mean "ignorance" – that is, ignorance of Islam. However, other scholars maintain that its original significance was wildness," "savagery," the opposite of *hilm* (moral reasonableness), rather than the opposite of *'ilm* (knowledge). See Reynold A Nicholson, *A Literary History of the Arabs* (Cambridge: The University Press, 1969, first pub. 1907), p. 30 and Ignaz Goldziher *Muhammedanische Studien*, Part I, p. 225.

4. See W. Robertson Smith, *Kinship and Marriage in Early Arabia*, (Boston: Beacon Press, n.d., first pub. 1903), pp. 28ff, for a discussion of arguments for the idea that early female kinship relations were prevalent in early Arabia.

5. An Arabic term denoting a localized kindered group within the tribe possessing a common group-name and often, though not always, close blood relationship. The word literally means "life" or "living."

6. Smith, p. 94.

7. From the word for "lord" or "owner." Smith, p. 92.

8. We have the example of Khadijah, the first wife of Muhammad, who was a rich widow when he married her and began assisting her in the management of her financial affairs.

9. Nicholson, p. 88.

10. *Ibid.*, pp. 91-92, 95.

11. A 'story taken from Abu al Faraj al Isfahani, *Kitab al Aghani*, IX, 182, and related in Nicholson, pp. 109-110. It is the story of 'Amr ibn Kulthum, one of the poets of the *Mu'allaqāt*, a collection of seven pre-Islamic odes which were probably compiled in the Umayyah period (before 750 A.C.).

12. See Nicholson, pp. 126-127.

13. For a fuller description of the *hanifs*, see Nicholson, pp. 149-150.

14. See Ibn Ishaq, pp. 66-68, for the story of the female diviner and Abd al Muttalib, the grandfather of Prophet Muhammad.

15. Asaf A. A. Fyzee, *Outlines of Muhammadan Law* (London: Oxford University Press, 1955, first pub. 1949), p. 74.

16. When a newly-married girl complained to the Prophet that her father had chosen her husband without consulting her, he immediately gave her permission to annul her marriage, to which she replied: 'I have no personal objection to my husband and I accept him, but I wanted it to be known that a father has no right to impose a husband upon his daughter without her consent.'" This is a *hadith* quoted by Saīd Ramadān, *Three Major Problems confronting the World of Islam* (Geneva: Islamic Center, 1961), p. 10.

17. Qur'ānic references in the text refer to the edition of Abdullah Yusuf 'Ali, *The Holy Qur'ān* (Washington, D.C.: The American International Printing Co., 1946, first pub. 1934). See also Fyzee, Chap. III, pp. 110-122.

18. Fyzee, pp. 99-101.

19. "... And women shall have rights similar to the rights against them..." (2:228).

20. Precedent for this is found in Qur'ān 2:229.

21. Precedent for *li'an* divorce is found in Qur'ān 24:6-9. See also Muhammad ibn Idris al Shafi'i, *Risala*, tr. Majid Khadduri, *Islamic Jurisprudence* (Baltimore: Johns Hopkins Press, 1961), Chap. VII, pp. 147-148.

22. From a tradition of Bukhari, quoted by Fyzee, p. 143.

23. See Qur'ān 4-34 for statement that men shall be responsible for supporting women.

24. Joseph Schacht, *An Introduction to Islamic Law* (Oxford: Clarendon Press, 1964), pp. 127-29.

25. Khalid M. Khalid, *Min Hina Nabda'*, tr. Isma'il R. al Faruqi, *Our Beginning in Wisdom* (Washington, D.C.: American Council of Learned Societies 1953), p. 113.

26. Fyzee, p. 403.

27. Muhammad al Ghazzali, *Min Huna Na'lam*, tr. Isma'il R. al Faruqi, *Our Beginning in Wisdom* (Washington, D.C.: American Council of Learned Societies, 1953), p. 113.

28. The "example" of the Prophet is recorded in vast collections of *hadith* literature which records sayings and actions attributed to Muhammad, *sallallahu alehi wasallam*, by Muslims of the early centuries of Islam and carefully verified by exhaustively compiled and substantiated *isnad*, the chains of carriers or relators of the various traditions, from the time of the Prophet to the time of its being recorded by the "traditionists" or masters of *hadith*.

29. See Fyzee, pp. 130-131, for "Disapproved Forms" of *talaq*.

30. *Ibid.*, pp. 172-74.

31. Every Muslim believes that the Qur'ān is not the creation of Muhammad, but the speech of God, revealed word by word to Muhammad His Prophet.

32. al Ghazzali, p. 111.

33. Germain Tillion, *Le harem et les cousins*, as quoted by David C Gordon, *Women of Algeria: An Essay on change* (Cambridge, Massachusetts: Harvard U. Press, 1968), pp. 6-9.

34 For other discrepancies between *shari'ah* and local customary law in Islamic countries, see N. J. Coulson, *A History of Islamic Law*, Vol. II of *Islamic Surveys* (Edinburgh: The University Press, 1964), pp. 135-138.

35. Mary Wollstonecraft's *Vindication of the Rights of Women* was written in 1792, John Stuart Mill's *The Subjection of Women* in 1867. In 1848 an organized feminist movement was born at a convention in Seneca Falls, New York, attended by Elizabeth Cady Stanton and Lucretia Mott.

36. Born in Afghanistan, al Afghani (1839-97) lived in British India, Makkah, and Constantinopole before becoming leader of reform movements in Egypt. He believed women has an equal natural endowment with men.

37. Muhammad 'Abduh (1849-1905) based his reform on a return to the basic principles of Islam. He argued for education of women and insisted that improvement of the condition of women was a necessary step toward Islamic society's social reform.

38. A disciple of Muhammad 'Abduh, Qasim Amin (1865-1908) lived and worked in Egypt. He wrote *The Emancipation of Women and The New Woman*.

39. See *The Tunisian Code of Personal Status (Majallat al Ahwal al Shakhsiyah)*, translated and reprinted in *The Middle East Journal*, XI, 1957, Book I, Article 18.

40. *The Tunisian Code of Personal Status*, Book II, Article 30.

41. Sh. Shaukat Mahmood, *Muslim Family Laws Ordinance*, 1961 (Lahore, W. Pakistan: Pakistan Law Times Publications, 1968, first pub. 1962), p. 27.

42. The Singapore Muslim's Ordinance, 1957, mentioned by J. N. D. Anderson, "The

Eclipse of the Patriarchal Family in Contemporary Islamic Law," *Family Law in Asia and Africa* ed. J. N. D. Anderson (New York: Frederick A. Praeger, 1968, first pub. 1967), p. 228. Another province of Malaya, Selangor, barred *talaq* without the approval of the *qadi* and the agreement of the wife in its rules relating to marriage and divorce in 1962. In the Singapore Muslim's Ordinance, 1957, a divorce can be registered only through the *qadi* and after he is satisfied that both husband and wife have consented (Ahmad Ibrahim, *Islamic Law in Malaya* (Singapore: Malaysian Sociological Research Institute, Ltd., 1965), p. 207.

43. In Turkey women had the vote from 1930; in Syria and Indonesia, from 1949; in Lebanon, from 1952; in Egypt and Pakistan, 1956; in Tunisia, 1957; in Malaya, 1959; in Algeria, 1962; in Iran, 1963; in Iraq, 1967. France gave women the vote only after World War II, and to this day the women of Switzerland do not vote.

44. *The Tunisian Code of Personal Status*, Book I, Article 24, says that the husband is not the guardian of the wife's property.

45. This took place at the primary level in 1960. Since then education in Saudi Arabia has become open to girls from kindergarten to the university level, though in restricted fields.

46. The number of girls in the schools of Egypt between the years 1921-22 and 1949-50 increased over twenty-fold (Nejla Izzeddin, *The Arab World Past, Present, and Future* (Chicago: Henry Regnery Company, 1953), p. 307. In Iraq, during the same period, the enrollment of girls in schools increased from 160 to over 44,000 (*Ibid.*, p. 308).

47. The following are the percentages of total enrollments according to sex in six Muslim countries. These statistics are taken from *Access of Women to Education*, The Fifteenth International Conference on Public Education convened by UNESCO and the I.B.E.
(Geneva: International Bureau of Education, 1952), Publication No. 141.

	Boys	Girls
Primary Schools (p. 17)		
Egypt	64.76	35.24
Iraq	75.31	24.69
Jordan	74.29	25.21
Persia	75.18	24.82
Syria	72.11	27.89
Turkey	62.47	37.52
Secondary Schools (p. 21)		
Egypt	90.25	9.75
Iraq	77.49	22.51
Jordan	82.05	17.95
Persia	78.53	21.65
Syria	75.21	24.29
Turkey	63.27	36.73
Higher Education		
Egypt	93.55	6.45
Iraq	83.42	16.58
Jordan		
Persia	97.27	273

| Syria | 81.27 | 18.73 |
| Turkey | 81.16 | 18.84 |

48. "Education is a sacred duty for every Muslim and every Muslimah." This is a *hadith* quoted by Muhammad Marmaduke Pickthall, *The Cultural Side of Islam* (Lahore, Pakistan: Sh. Muhammad Ashraf, 1969, first pub. 1961), p. 142.

Chapter II

Islamic Traditions and The Feminist Movement: Confrontation or Cooperation?

Whether living in the Middle East or Africa, in Central Asia, in Pakistan, in Southeast Asia, or in Europe and the Americas, Muslim women tend to view the feminist movement with some apprehension. Although there are some features of the feminist cause with which we as Muslims would wish to join hands, other features generate our disappointment and even opposition. There is therefore no simple or "pat" answer to the question of the future cooperation or competition which feminism may meet in an Islamic environment.

There are however a number of social, psychological, and economic traditions which govern the thinking of most Muslims and which are particularly affective of woman's status and role in Islamic society. Understanding these can help us understand the issues which affect male and female status and roles, and how we should react to movements which seek to improve the situation of women in any of the countries where Muslims live.

The Family System: One of the Islamic traditions which will affect the way in which Muslim women respond to feminist ideas is the advocacy in Islamic culture of an extended rather than a nuclear family system. Some Muslim families are "residentially extended" – that is, their members live communally with three or more generations of relatives (grandparents, parents, uncles, aunts, and their offspring) in a single building or compound. Even where this residential version of the extended family is not possible or adhered to, family connections reaching far beyond the nuclear unit are evident in strong psychological, social, economic and even political ties. Mutual supports and responsibilities affecting these larger consanguine groups are not just considered desirable, but they are made legally incumbent on members of the society by Islamic law. The Holy Qur'ān itself exhorts to extended family solidarity; in addition it specifies the extent of such responsibilities and contains prescriptive measures for inheritance, support, and other close interdependencies within the extended family.[1]

Our Islamic traditions also prescribe a much stronger participation of the family in the contracting and preservation of marriages. While most Western feminists would decry family participation or arranged marriage as a negative influence because of its apparent restriction of individualistic freedom and responsibility, as Muslims we would argue that such participation is advantageous for both individuals and groups within the society. Not only does it ensure marriages based on sounder principles than physical attraction and sexual infatuation, but it provides other safeguards for successful marital continuity. Members of the family provide diverse companionship as well as ready sources of advice and sympathy for the newly married as they adjust to each others' way. One party of the marriage cannot easily pursue an eccentric course at the expense of the spouse since such behavior would rally opposition from the larger group. Quarrels are never so devastating to the marriage bond since other adult family members act as mediators and provide altenative sources of companionship and cousel following disagreements. The problems of parenting and generational incompatability are also alleviated, and singles clubs and dating bureaus would be unnecessary props for social interaction. There is no need in the extended family for children of working parents to be unguarded, unattended, or inadequately loved and socialized because the extended family home is never empty. There is therefore no feeling of guilt which the working parent often feels in a nuclear of single-parent organization. Tragedy, even divorce, is not so debilitating to either adults or children since the larger social unit absorbs the residual numbers with much greater ease than a nuclear family organization can ever provide.

The move away from the cohesiveness which the family formerly enjoyed in Western society, the rise of usually smaller alternative family styles, and the accompanying rise in individualism which many feminists advocate or at least practice, are at odds with these deep-rooted Islamic customs and traditions. If feminism in the Muslim world chooses to espouse the Western family models, it should and would certainly be strongly challenged by Muslim women's groups and by Islamic society as a whole.

Individualism vs. the Larger Organization: The traditional support of the large and intricately interrelated family orgnization is correlative to another Islamic tradition which seems to run counter to recent Western trends and to feminist ideology. Islam and Muslim women generally advocate molding of individual goals and interests to accord with the welfare of the larger group and its members. Instead of holding the goals of the individual supreme, Islam instills in the adherent a sense of his or her place within the family and of a responsibility to that group. This is not perceived or experienced by Muslims as repression of the individual. Other traditions which will be discussed later guarantee his or her legal personality. Feminism, therefore, would not be espoused by Muslim women as a goal to be pursued without regard for the relation of the female to the other members of her family. The Muslim woman regards her goals as necessitating a balance with, or even subordination to, those of the family group. The rampant individualism often experienced in contemporary life, that which treats the goals of the individual in isolation from other factors, or as utterly supreme, runs against a deep Islamic commitment to social interdependence.

Differentiation of Sex Roles: A third Islamic tradition which affects the future of any feminist movement in an Islamic environment is that it specifies a differentiation of male and female roles and responsibilities in society. Feminism, as represented in Western society, has generally denied any such differentiation and has demanded a move toward a unisex society in order to achieve equal rights for women. By "unisex society," I mean one in which a single set of roles and concerns are given preference and esteem by both sexes and are pursued by all members of the society regardless of sex and age differentials. In the case of Western feminism, the preferred goals have been those traditionally fulfilled by the male members of society. The roles of providing financial support, of success in career, and of decision making have been given overwhelming respect and concern while those dealing with domestic matters, with child care, with aesthetic and psychological refreshment, with social interrelationships, were devalued and even despised. Both men and women have been forced into a single mold which is perhaps more restrictive, rigid and coercive than that which formerly assigned men to one type of role and women to another.

This is a new brand of male chauvinism with which Islamic traditions cannot conform. Islam instead maintains that both types of roles are equally deserving of pursuit and respect and that when accompanied by the equity demanded by the religion, a division of labor along sex lines is generally beneficial to all members of the society.

This might be regarded by the feminist as opening the door to discrimination, but as Muslims we regard Islamic traditions as standing clearly and unequivocally for the support of Male-female equity. In the Qur'ān, no difference whatever is made between the sexes in relation to God. "For men who submit [to God] and for women who submit [to God], for believing men and believing women, for devout men and devout women, for truthful men and truthful women, for steadfast men and steadfast women, for humble men and humble women, for charitable men and charitable women, for men who fast and women who fast, for men who guard their chastity and women who guard, for men who remember God much and for women who remember – for them God has prepared forgiveness and a mighty reward" (33:35). "Whoever performs good deeds, whether male or female, and is a believer, We shall surely make him live a good life and We will certainly reward them for the best of what they did" (16:97).[2]

It is only in relation to each other and society that a difference is made – a difference of role or function. The rights and responsibilities of a woman are equal to those of a man, but they are not necessarily identical with them. Equality and identity are two different things, Islamic traditions maintain – the former desirable, the latter not. Men and women should therefore be complementary to each other in a multi-function organization rather than competitive with each other in a uni-function society.

The equality demanded by Islamic traditions must, however, be seen in its larger context if it is to be understood properly. Since Muslims regard a differentiation of sexual roles to be natural and desirable in the majority of cases, the economic responsibilities of male and female members differ to provide a balance for the physical differences between men and women and for the greater responsibility which women carry in the reproductive and rearing activities so necessary to the well-being of the society. To maintain, therefore, that the men of the family are responsible for providing economically for the women or that women are not equally responsible, is not a dislocation or denial of sexual equity. It is instead a duty to be fulfilled by men as compensation for another responsibility which involves the special ability of women. Likewise the different inheritance rate for males and females, which is so often cited as an example of discrimination against women, must not be seen as an isolated prescription. It is but one part of a comprehensive system in which women carry no legal reponsibility to support other members of the family, but in which men are bound by law as well as custom to provide for all their female relatives.

Does this mean that Islamic traditions necessarily prescribe maintaining the status quo in the Islamic societies that exist today? The answer is a definite "No." Many thinking Muslims – both men and women – would agree that their societies do not fulfill the Islamic ideals and traditions laid down in the Qur'ān and reinforced by the example and directives of the Prophet Muhammad, *sallallahu alehi wasallam*. It is reported in the Qur'ān and from history that women not only expressed their opinions freely in the Prophet's presence, but also argued and participated in serious discussions with the Prophet himself and with other Muslim leaders of the time (58:1). Muslim women are known to have even stood in opposition to certain caliphs, who later accepted the sound arguments of those women. A specific example took place during the caliphate of 'Umar ibn al Khattab.' The Qur'ān reproached those who believed woman to be inferior to men (16:57-59) and repeatedly gives expression to the need for treating men and women with equity (2:228, 231; 4:19, and so on). Therefore, if Muslim women experience discrimination in any place or time, they do not and should not lay the blame on Islam, but on the un-Islamic nature of their societies and the failure of Muslims to fulfill its directives.

Separate Legal Status for Women: A fourth Islamic tradition affecting the future of feminism in Muslim societies is the separate legal status for women which is demanded by the Qur'ān and the *Shari'ah*. Every Muslim individual, whether male or female, retains a separate identity from cradle to grave. This separate legal personality prescribes for every woman the right to contract, to conduct business, to earn and possess property independently. Marriage has no effect on her legal status, her property, her earnings – or even on her name. If she commits any civil offense, her penalty is no less or no more than a man's in a similar case (5:83; 24:2). If she is wronged or harmed, she is entitled to compensation just like a man (4:92-93; see also Mustafa al Sibā'i 1976:38; Darwāzah n.d.:78). The feminist demand for separate legal status for women is therefore one that is equally espoused by Islamic traditions.

Polygyny: Although the taking of plural wives by a man is commonly called polygamy, the more correct sociological designation is polygyny. This institution is probably the Islamic tradition most misunderstood and vehemently condemned by non-Muslims. It is one which the Hollywood stereotypes "play upon" in their ridicule of Islamic society. The first image conjured up in the mind of the Westerner when the subject of Islam and marriage is approached is that of a religion which advocates the sexual indulgence of the male members of the society and the subjugation of its females through this institution.

Islamic tradition does indeed allow a man to marry more than one woman at a time. This leniency is even established by the Qur'ān (4:3).[5] But the use and perception of that institution is far from the Hollywood stereotype. Polygyny is certainly not imposed by Islam; nor is it a universal practice. It is instead regarded as the exception to the norm of monogamy, and its exercise is strongly controlled by social pressures.[6] If utilized by Muslim men to facilitate or condone sexual promiscuity, it is not less Islamically condemnable than serial polygyny and adultery, and no less detrimental to the society. Muslims view polygyny as an institution which is to be called into use only under extraordinary circumstances. As such, it has not been generally regarded by Muslim women as a threat. Attempts by the feminist movement to focus on eradication of this institution in order to improve the status of women would therefore meet with little sympathy or support.

II. Directives for the Feminist Movement in an Islamic Environment

What can be learned about the future compatibility or incongruity of feminism in a Muslim environment from these facts about Islamic traditions? Are there any general principles to be gained, any directives to be taken, by those who work for women's rights and human rights in the world?

Intercultural Incompatibility of Western Feminism: The first and foremost principle would seem to be that many of the goals of feminism as conceived in Western society are not necessarily relevant or exportable across cultural boundaries. Feminism as a Western movement originated in England during the 18th century and had as one of its main goals the eradication of legal disabilities imposed upon women by English common law. These laws were especially discriminatory of married women. They derived in part from Biblical sources (e.g., the idea of man and woman becoming "one flesh," and the attribution of an inferior and even evil nature to Eve and all her female descendants) and in part from feudal customs (e.g., the importance of carrying and supplying arms for battle and the concommitant devaluation of the female contributions to society). The Industrial Revolution and its need for women's contribution to the work force brought strength to the feminist movement and helped its advocates gradually break down most of those discriminatory laws.

Since the history and heritage of the Muslim peoples have been radically different from that of Western Europe and America, the feminism which would appeal to Muslim women and to the society generally must be correspondingly different. Those legal rights which Western women sought in reform of English common law were already granted to Muslim women in the 7th century. Such a struggle therefore holds little interest for the Muslim woman. In addition, it would be useless to try to interest us in ideas or reforms that run in diametrical opposition to those traditions which form an important part of our cultural and religious heritage. There has been a good deal of opposition to any changes in Muslim personal status laws since these embody and reinforce the very traditions which we have been discussing. In other words, if feminism is to succeed in an Islamic environment, it must be an indigenous form of feminism, rather than one conceived and nurtured in an alien environment with different problems and different solutions and goals.

The Form of an Islamic Feminism: If the goals of Western feminism are not viable for Muslim women, what form should a feminist movement take to ensure success?

Above all, the movement must recognize that, whereas in the West, the mainstream of the women's movement has viewed religion as one of the chief enemies of its progress and well-being, Muslim women view the teachings of Islam as their best friend and supporter. The prescriptions that are found in the Qur'ān and in the example of the Prophet Muhammad, *sallallahu alehi wasallam*, are regarded as the ideal to which contemporary women wish to return. As far as Muslim women are concerned, the source of any difficulties experienced today is not Islam and its traditions, but certain alien ideological intrusions on our societies, ignorance, and distortion of the true Islam, or exploitation by individuals within the society. It is a lack of an appreciation for this fact that caused such misunderstanding and mutual distress when women's movement representatives from the West visited Iran both before and after the Islamic Revolution.

Second, any feminism which is to succeed in an Islamic environment must be one which does not work chauvinistically for women's interest alone. Islamic traditions would dictate that women's progress be achieved in tandem with the wider struggle to benefit all members of the society. The good of the group or totality is always more crucial than the good of any one sector of the society. In fact, the society is seen as an organic whole in which the welfare of each member or organ is necessary for the health and well being of every other part. Disadvantageous circumstances of women therefore should always be countered in conjunction with attempt to alleviate those factors which adverely affect men and other segments of the society.

Third, Islam is an ideology which influences much more than the ritual life of a people. It is equally affective of their social, political, economic, psychological, and aesthetic life. *"Din,"* which is usually regarded as an equivalent for the English term "religion," is a concept which includes, in addition to those ideas and practices customarily associated in our minds with religion, a wide spectrum of practices and ideas which affect almost every aspect of the daily life of the Muslim individual. Islam and Islamic traditions therefore are seen today by many Muslims as the main source of cohesiveness for nurturing an identity and stability to confront intruding alien influences and the cooperation needed to solve their numerous contemporary problems. To fail to note this fact, or to fail to be fully appreciative of its importance for the average Muslim – whether male or female – would be to commit any movement advocating improvement of women's position in Islamic lands to certain failure. It is only through establishing that identity and stability that self-respect can be achieved and a more healthy climate for both Muslim men and Muslim women will emerge.

Notes

1. For example, see Qur'ān 2:177; 4:7, 176; 8:41; 16:90; 17:26; 24:22.

2. See also Qur'ān 2:195; 4:124, 32; 9:71-72.
3. "God (thus) directs you as regards your children's (inheritance): to the male, a proportion equal to that of two females..." (Qur'ān 4:11).
4. Kamal 'Awn 1955:129.
5. "... Marry women of your choice, two, or three, or four; but if you fear that you shall not be able to deal justly (with them), then only one, or (a captive) that your right hands possess. That will be more suitable, to prevent you from doing injustice."
6. It should be remembered that any woman who wants her marriage to remain monogamous can provide for this condition under Islamic law.

References

Kamal Ahmad 'Awn, *Al Mar'ah fi al Islam* (Tanta: Sha'rawi Press, 1955).

Muhammad 'Izzat Darwāzah, *Al Dustur al Qur'āni fi Shu'ūn al Hayāt* (Cairo: 'Isa al Babi al Halabi, n.d.).

Mustafa al Siba'i, *Al Mar'ah baynal Fiqh wal Qanun* (Aleppo: Al Maktabah al 'Arabiyyah, first pub. 1962).

Chapter III

Women in a Qur'ānic Society

T he topic of this paper was chosen out of the conviction that humanity is suffering today from a number of serious social problems related to women and to the interrelations of the two sexes in society. Although these problems may be more pronounced, more disturbing, more debilitating for some of us than for others, there are probably few if any regions of the contemporary world whose citizens have not felt in some way the repercussions of these problems. Therefore, there is a pressing need for exploring possible solutions. The problem of women is linked, for the present study, with the Qur'ān, and what I have called the "Qur'ānic society," out of strong conviction that the Qur'an offers the most viable guidance for contemporary social reform which can be found in any model or any literature.

Many of you may be puzzled by the title of this paper – "Women in a Qur'ānic Society." You may ask yourselves, "Why didn't she say "Women in Muslim Society" or even "Women in an Islamic Society?" Let me explain why the expressions "Muslim" and "Islamic" were rejected for this paper, and how the use of the rather unusual appellation, "Qur'ānic society," is justified.

There are at least three reasons for my choice of that title. The first of these derives from the concern that many beliefs and practices have been labelled "Muslim" or "Islamic" without warranting those names. There are approximately 40 nations of the world which claim to have a Muslim majority population and therefore to be exemplary of "Muslim" or "Islamic" societies. This of course results in a great deal of confusion as the question is asked: Which of these regions represents most faithfully the true "Islamic" society? Among Muslims that question is most frequently answered by the claim that their own national or regional society is the truest to the intentions of Allah *subhānahu wa ta'āla*.

Non-Muslims, on the other hand, and especially the Western anthropologists who travel around the world to investigate the customs and mores of its peoples, tend to treat each variation within the Muslim World as equally valid. This results from their adherence to what I call the "zoo theory" of knowledge. Adherents of that theory regard all Muslims – and of course similar treatment of other non-Western people is discernible – as different species within the human zoo. The "zoo theory" protagonists go to the field, record and snap pictures of every strange or exotic practice they see and hear; and for them, this is Islam or Islamic practice. A trip to another part of the Muslim World with the ubiquitous devices for recording and photographing generates a different body of materials documenting superficial variations in customs. But this, too, is Islam or Islamic practice for the "zoo theory" investigator or ethnographer. There is far too little effort spent on understanding Islam as a whole. As a result, the basic premise of skepticism and relativism is confirmed in the mind of the researcher; and he or she returns home convinced that there is not one Islam, but scores of Islams existent in the world. In like fashion, the researcher reports that there are many definitions or descriptions of the status and role of women in Muslim society. Each one of the resultant definitions or descriptions is dubbed as "Muslim" or "Islamic," even if we as Muslims may hold some of these practices to be distortions or perversions of our principles and beliefs by the misguided or uninformed among us.

It was partly to avoid confusion with these variant descriptions and misunderstandings that I have chosen the appellation "Qur'ānic" for the present discussion. In this way, I hope to move beyond the limited relevance and particularism of a "zoo theory" of investigation to a presentation which avoids such fragmentation and is ideologically in conformance with the true prescriptions of Islam. In regard to matters so determining of our destiny and very existence, we can never be satisfied with mere reportage about certain human animals in the "zoo" who are statistically "Muslim" or whose customs have been labelled as "Islamic." Those designations have sometimes been misapplied. "Qur'ānic," on the other hand, is a term which is unequivocal. It points clearly to the topic of this paper.

Second, "Qur'ānic society" was judged to be the most suitable title for it orients us toward discovering those core principles in the Qur'ān itself which form the underlying framework for our societies throughout the Muslim World. It is the society based on Qur'ānic principles which is the goal of all of us, even though we may unknowingly deviate from time to time from those principles. It is the conformance to a Qur'ān-based society for which we must all work if the Muslim peoples are to enjoy a felicitous future. It is not an

Indonesian, Pakistani, Saudi Arabian, Egyptian or Nigerian version of that society that we should regard as indisputable norm, but one firmly based on the teachings of the Holy Qur'ān. Only therein can we find a proper definition of woman's role in society. Since it is these teachings which are the subject of my paper, "Women in a Qur'ānic Society" seemed the most proper title.

Third, I wish by this choice of title to emphasize that we should regard the Holy Qur'ān as our guide in all aspect of our lives. It is not only the prime source of knowledge about religious beliefs, obligations, and practices, it is also the guide, whether specific or implied, for every aspect of Islamic civilization. In the centuries of past glory, it determined the political, economic, social, and artistic creativity of the Muslim peoples. If we are to succeed as members of an Islamic society in the coming decades and centuries, it must again determine our thinking and our actions in all-inclusive way. Islam is not limited to the Five Pillars of the *shahādah, salāh, siyām, zakāh,* and the *hajj.* Islam in fact defies simple equation with the English term "religion," for the former's significance penetrates into every nook and cranny of human existence and behavior. Surely it should be our goal to relate every action to our Islam. We can only do this by allowing the Holy Qur'ān to in-form and re-form every realm of our lives.

As a step in this direction, let us consider what the Qur'ān has to teach us about the society toward which we should be striving and ponder its effect on the position of women. What are the basic characteristics of a Qur'ānic society which particularly affect women?

Five characteristics – which seem basic, crucial and incontrovertible – of Qur'ānic society will be considered. Although they are presented in a series, each rests upon the others and affects them. The interdependence of these five characteristics makes it difficult to speak of any one of them without mention of the others, and of course they do not and cannot exist in isolation from one another.

1. Equal Status and Worth of the Sexes

The first of these characteristics of a Qur'ānic society which affect women is that both sexes are held to be equal in status and worth. In other words, the Qur'ān teaches us that women and men are all creatures of Allah, existing on a level of equal worth and value, although their equal importance does not substantiate a claim for their equivalence or perfect identity. This equality of male and female is documentable in the Qur'ān in passages pertaining to at least four aspects of human existence and interaction.

Religious Matters

The first of these Qur'ānic confirmations of male-female equality are contained in statements pertaining to such religious matters as the origins of humanity, or to religious obligations and rewards.

Origins of Humanity: The Qur'ān is devoid of the stories found in the Old Testament which denigrate women. There is no hint that the first woman created by God is a creature of lesser worth than the first male, or that she is a kind of appendage formed from one of his ribs. Instead, male and female are created, we read, *min nafsin wāhidatin* ("from a single soul or self") to complement each other (4:1; 7:189). Whereas the Torah or Old Testament treats Eve as the temptress of the Garden of Eden, who aids Satan in enticing Adam to disobey God, the Qur'ān deals with the pair with perfect equity. Both are equally guilty of sinning; both are equally punished by God with expulsion from the Garden; and both are equally forgiven when they repent.

Religious Obligations and Rewards: The Qur'ān is not less clear in commanding equality for men and women in its directives regarding religious obligations and rewards. We read:

Lo! Men who surrender unto Allah, and women who surrender, and men who believe and women who believe, and men who obey and women who obey, and men who speak the truth and women who speak the truth, and men who persevere (in righteousness) and women who persevere, and men who are humble and women who are humble, and men who give alms and women who give alms, and men who fast and women who fast, and men who guard their modesty and women who guard (their modesty), and men who remember Allah and women who remember — Allah has prepared for them forgiveness and a vast reward. (33:35)[1]

Ethical Obligations and Rewards: The Qur'ān reveals to mankind the desired equality of the two sexes by establishing the same ethical obligations and rewards for women and men.

And whoever does good works, whether male or female, and he

(or she) is a believer, such will enter Paradise and they will not be wronged the dint in a date-stone (4:124).

Whoever does right, whether male or female, and is a believer, him – verily We shall quicken with good life, and We shall pay them a recompense according to the best of what they do (16:97).[2]

If Allah the Exalted had not deemed the two sexes of equal status and value, such explicit statements of their equality in ethical obligations and rewards would not have been made in the Qur'ān.

Education: Although the more specific commands for the equal rights of women and men to pursue education can be found in the *hadīth* literature, the Qur'ān does at least imply the pursuit of knowledge by all Muslims regardless of their sex. For example, it repeatedly commands all readers to read, to recite, to think, to contemplate, as well as to learn from the signs (*āyāt*) of Allah in nature. In fact, the very first revelation to Prophet Muhammad, *sallallāhu alehi wasallam*, was concerned with knowledge. In a Qur'ānic society, there can never be a restriction of this knowledge to one sex. It is the duty of every Muslim and every Muslimah to pursue knowledge throughout life, even if it should lead the seeker to China, we are told.[3] The Prophet even commanded that the slave girls be educated,[4] and he asked Shifā' bint 'Abdillāh to instruct his wife Hafsah bint 'Umar.[5] Lectures of the Prophet were attended by audiences of both men and women; and by the time of the Prophet's death, there were many women scholars.[6]

Legal Rights: A fourth evidence in the Qur'ān for the equality of men and women is its specification of legal rights which are guaranteed for every individual from cradle to grave. Unlike the situation in the West, where until the last century it was impossible for a married woman to hold property on her own, to contract with other persons, or to dispose of her property without the consent of her husband,[7] the Qur'ān proclaims the right of every woman to buy and sell, to contract and to earn,[8] and to hold and manage her own money and property. In addition to these rights, the Qur'ān grants woman a share in the inheritance of the family (4:7,11), warns against depriving her of that inheritance (4:19), specifies that the dower (*mahr*) of her marriage should belong to her alone and never be taken by her husband (2:229; 4:19-21, 25) unless offered by the woman as a free gift (4:44).[9]

As with any privilege, these rights of women carry corresponding responsibilities. If she commits a civil offence, the Qur'ān tells us, woman's penalty is no less or no more than that of a man in a similar case (5:41; 24:2). If she is wronged or harmed, she is entitled to compensation just like a man.[10]

It is clear that the Qur'ān not only recommends, but is even insistent upon, the equality of women and men as an essential characteristic of a Qur'ānic society. The claim of the non-Muslim critics that Islam denigrates women is denied emphatically by the Qur'ān. Similarly denied are the arguments of certain Muslims that women are religiously, intellectually and ethically inferior to men, as Jewish and Christian literatures had earlier maintained.

II. A Dual Sex Rather Than Unisex Society

Now let us consider the second basic characteristic of the Qur'ānic society which affects the position of women. This is found in the directives for a dual sex rather than a unisex society. While maintaining the validity of the equal worth of men and women, the Qur'ān does not judge this equality to mean equivalence or identity of the sexes.

Probably all of you are familiar with the contemporary move toward unisex clothes and shoes, unisex jewelry and hair styles, unisex actions and entertainments. In fact, it is often difficult in America to decide whether one is looking at a boy or a girl. This results from the current notion in Western society that there is little if any difference between the two sexes in physical, intellectual, and emotional endowment; and that, therefore, there should be no difference in their functions and roles in society.[11] The dress and the actions are but superficial evidence of this deeper conviction. Accompanied by a downgrading of the qualities and roles traditionally associated with the female sex, this current idea has generated a unisex society in which only the male role is respected and pursued. Although meant to bring a larger measure of equality for women, the idea that men and women are not only equal, but equivalent and identical, has actually pushed women into imitating men and even despising their womanhood. Thus, it is generating a new type of male chauvinism. Tremendous social pressures have resulted in stripping women of their role-responsibilites formerly performed by them, and they are forced to live a life devoid of personality and individuality.

The society based on the Qur'ān is, in contrast, a dual-sex society in which both sexes are assigned their special responsibilities. This assures the healthy functioning of the society for the benefit of all its members. This division of labor imposes on men more economic reponsibilities (2:233, 240; 4:34), while women are expected to play their role in childbearing and rearing (2:233; 7:189). The Qur'ān, recognizing the importance of this complementary sexual assignment of roles and responsibilities, alleviates the greater economic demands made on male members of the population by allotting them a larger share than women in inheritance. At the same time, it grants women the right to maintenance in exchange for her contribution to the physical and emotional well being of the family and to the care she provides in the rearing of children. The unisex ideology generates a competitive relationship between the sexes which we find in America and which is disastrous for all members of society: the young; the old; the children; the parents; the single and the married; the male and the female. The dual-sex society, by contrast, is a more natural answer to the question of sexual relationships, encouraging cooperation rather than competition between the sexes. It is a plan which has been found suitable in countless societies through history. Only in very recent times did the idea of sexual non-differentiation or identity achieve prominence, and then primarily in the Western society. Even the medical evidence for mental or emotional difference between the sexes is suppressed in Western research, for it threatens the prevailing trends of thought. How long this socially disastrous movement will continue before it is rejected as bankrupt is not known. But certainly we as Muslims should be aware of its deficiencies and dangerous consequences, and make our societies and young people aware of the disaster caused by it.

Protagonists of the unisex society have condemned the dual-sex human organization as dangerous for the well-being of women. If dual sex means that one sex is superior to the other, such a situation could have arisen. But in the true Qur'ānic society, toward which we all aspire to move, this is not possible. As we have seen above, the Qur'ān advocates eloquently the equal status of women and men at the same time as it recognizes their generally relevant differences of nature and function. Thus while acknowledging the religious, ethical, intellectual, and legal equality of males and females, the Qur'ān never regards the two sexes as identical or equivalent. It justifies this stand in its assignment of variant responsibilities and its provisions concerning inheritance and maintenance which match those responsibilities.

III. Interdependence of the Members of Society

The third characteristic of the Qur'ānic society which is strongly assertive of women's position is the insistence on the interdependence of the members of society. Contrary to the contemporary trend to emphasize the rights of the individual at the expense of society, we find the Qur'ān repeatedly emphasizing the interdependence of the male and female as well as of all members of society. The wife and husband, for example, are described as "garments" (*libās*) of each other (2:187), and as mates living and dwelling in tranquility (33:21; see also 7:189). Men and women are directed to complement each other (9:71). Each is called upon to fulfil certain assigned responsibilities for the good of both and the larger group.

In order to insure this interdependence which is so necessary for the physical and psychological well-being of both men and women, Allah, in the Holy Qur'ān, stipulated the reciprocal or mutual duties and obligations of the various members of the family – men and women, fathers and mothers, children and elders, and relatives of all degrees (17:23-26; 4:1, 7-12; 2:177; 8:41; 16:90; etc.). The care of and concern for other members of society is equally a duty of the Muslim:

> It is not righteousness that you turn faces to the east and the west; but righteous is he who believes in Allah and the Last Day and the angels and the Scripture and the prophets; and gives his wealth, for love of Him, to kinsfolk and to orphans and the needy and the wayfarer and to those who ask, and to set slaves free... (2:177)

The Qur'ān thereby instils in the Muslim a sense of a place within, and responsibility to society. This is not regarded or experienced as a repression of the individual. Instead, the Muslim is constantly encouraged in this interdependence by experiencing the benefits it brings. The economic, social, and psychological advantages of such close relationships and concerns within the social group provide more than ample compensation for the individual to sublimate his/her individualistic aspirations. The anonymity and lack of social interdependence among its members in contemporary Western society have caused many serious problems. Loneliness, inadequate care of the aged, the generation gap, high suicide rates, and juvenile crime can all be traced back to the ever-worsening breakdown of social interdependence and the denial of the human necessity for mutual care.

IV. The Extended Family

Closely intertwined with interdependence is the fourth basic characteristic of the Qur'ānic society which serves to improve male-female relations. This is the institution of the extended family. In addition to the members of the nucleus that constitutes the family – mother, father, and their children – the Islamic family or *'ā'ilah* also includes grandparents, uncles, aunts, and their offspring. Normally Muslim families are "residentially extended" – that is, their members live communally with three or more generations of relatives in a single building or compound. Even where this residential version of the extended family is not possible or adhered to, family connections reaching far beyond the nuclear unit are evident in strong psychological, social, economic, and even political ties.

The extended family solidarity is prescribed and strengthened by the Holy Qur'ān, where we find repeated references to the rights of kin (17:23-26; 4:7-9; 8:41; 24:22; etc.) and the importance of treating them with kindness (2:83; 16:90; etc.). Inheritance portions, for not only the nuclear family members but those of the extended family as well, are specifically prescribed (2:180-182; 4:33,176). Dire punishment is threatened for those who ignore those measures for intra-family support (4:7-12). The extended family of Islamic culture is thus not merely a product of social conditions, it is an institution anchored in the word of God Himself and buttressed by His advice and rules.

The extended family is an institution which can provide tremendous benefits for both women and men when it exists in conjunction with the other basic characteristics of a Qur'ānic society.

1. It guards against the selfishness or eccentricity of any one party, since the individual faces not a single spouse but a whole family of peers, elders, and children if he or she goes "off course."

2. It allows for careers for women without detriment to themselves, spouse, children or elders, since there are always other adults in the home to assist the working wife or mother. Career women in an Islamic extended family suffer neither the physical and emotional burden of overwork nor the feeling of guilt for neglecting mat-

ernal, marital, or familial responsibilities. In fact, without this sort of family institution, it is impossible to imagine any feasible solution for the problems now facing Western society. As more and more women enter the work force, the nuclear family is unable to sustain the needs of its members. The difficulties in the single parent family are of course magnified a hundredfold. The strain that such family systems put on the working woman are devastating to the individual as well as to the marriage and family bonds. The dissolutions of families which result and psychological and social ramifications of the high divorce rate in America and other Western nations[12] are the growing concern of doctors, lawyers, psychiatrists, and sociologists as well as, of course, of the unfortunate victims of these phenomena.

3. The extended family insures the adequate socialization of children. A mother's or father's advice in a nuclear or single parent family may be difficult to be followed by an unruly or obstinate child, but the combined pressure of the members of a strong extended family is an effective counter to nonconformance or disobedience.

4. The extended family provides for psychological and social diversity in companionship for adults as well as children. Since there is less dependence on the one-to-one relationship, there are less emotional demands on each member of the family. A disagreement or clash between adults, children or between persons of different generations does not reach the damaging proportions it may in the nuclear family. There are always alternative family members on hand to ease the pain and provide therapeutic counselling and companionship. Even the marriage bond is not put to the enormous strains that it suffers in the nuclear family.

5. The extended family or *'ā'ilah* guards against the development of the generation gap. This social problem arises when each age group becomes so isolated from other generations that it finds difficulty in achieving successful and meaningful interaction with people of a different age level. In the *'ā'ilah*, three or more generations live together and constantly interact with one another. This situation provides beneficial learning and socialization experiences for children and the necessary sense of security and usefulness for the older generation.

6. The *'ā'ilah* eliminates the problems of loneliness which plague the isolated and anonymous dwellers in the urban centers of many contemporary societies. The unmarried woman, or the divorced or

widowed woman in an Islamic extended family will never suffer the problems that face such women in contemporary American society, for example. In a Qur'ānic society, there is no need for the commercial computer dating establishments, the singles' clubs and bars, or the isolation of senior citizens in retirement villages or old people's homes. The social and psychological needs of the individual, whether male or female, are cared for in the extended family.

As marriage bonds grow more and more fragile in Western society, women tend to be the chief victims of the change. They are less able to reestablish marriage or other bonds than men, and they are more psychologically damaged by these losses.

7. The extended family provides a more feasible and humane sharing of the care of the elderly. In the nuclear family unit, the care of the elderly parent or parents of one spouse may fall entirely on one individual, usually the mother of the family. She must provide for the extra physical care as well as for the emotional well-being of the elderly. This is a tremendous burden on a woman who probably has children's and husband's needs to attend to as well. If she is a working mother, the burden can be unmanageable; and the elderly are put in an old peoples' home to await death. With the shared responsibilities and duties that the extended family provides, the burden is significantly lightened.

V. A Patriarchal Family Organization

The fifth basic characteristic of a Qur'ānic society is that it is patriarchal. Contrary to the goals of the Women's Liberation movement, the Qur'ān calls for a society which assigns the ultimate leadership and decision-making role in the family to men.

Any society is made up of smaller organizations of humans – governments, political parties, religious organizations, commerical enterprises, extended families, and so on. Each of these organs needs to be stable, cohesive, and maneuverable if it is to be beneficial to its constituents. In order to acquire these characteristics, the organization must assign ultimate responsibility to some individual or some group within its ranks.

Therefore, the citizens may vote, parliament may legislate, and the police may enforce the law; but it is ultimately the head of state that carries the burden of making the crucial decisions for the nation, as well as the onus or approval – that is, the responsibility for those decisions. In like manner, the work of a factory is conducted by many individuals, but all of them are not equally capable of making the ultimate decisions for the company. Neither is each employee equally charged with the responsibility for the organization's success or failure.

The family also has need for someone to carry the burden of ultimate responsibility for the whole. The Qur'ān has assigned this role to the most senior male member of the family. It is this patriarchal assignment of power and responsibility which is meant by such expressions as وَلِلرِّجَالِ عَلَيْهُنَّ دَرَجَة "wa lil rijāl 'alayhinna darajatun" (2:228), and الرِّجَالُ قَوَّامُونَ عَلَى النِّسَاء "al-rijālu qawwāmūna 'alā al-nisā'i..." (4:34). Contrary to misrepresentations by the Qur'ān's enemies, these passages do not mean the subjugation of women to men in a gender-based dictatorship. Such an interpretation shows a blatant disregard of the Qur'ān's repeated calls for the equality of the sexes and for its command to show respect and kindness to women. The passages in question point instead to a means for avoiding internal dissension and indecision for the benefit of all family members. They advocate for a patriarchal society.

In addition, we would draw attention to the use of the word
    qawwāmūn in the statement, "al-rijālu qawwāmūna 'ala al-nisā'i..." (4:34). Certainly the verb "qawwama," from which the verbal noun "qawwāmūn" is derived, does not imply despotic overlordship. Instead, the term refers to the one who stands up (from qāma, "to stand") for another in a protective and benevolent way. If an autocratic or domineering role for the male half of the society had been meant, there are many other verbal derivatives which would have been more applicable, for example, مُسَيْطِرُون "musaytirūn" and مُهَيْمِنُون "muhayminūn." Other instances of the Qur'ānic use of the term qawwāmūn confirm this supportive rather than authoritarian or tyrannical meaning of the term (see 4:127-135; 5:9). Ascription of a different significance to the passage in question is, therefore, ideologically inconsistent as well as linguistically unsupportable.

Why should the Qur'ān specify male leadership for the 'ā'ilah – that is, a patriarchal family, rather than a matriarchal organization? The Qur'ān answers that question in the following manner:

> Men are in charge of women, because Allah has made the one of them to excel the other, and because they spend of their property (for the support of women) ... (4:34).

Physical and economic contributions and responsibility are, therefore, the Qur'ānic reasons for proposing a patriarchal rather than a matriarchal society.

Some Westerners, confronted by the problems of contemporary society, are beginning to ask such questions as: Where can we turn for help? What can we do in the face of the present social disintegration? It is a time of despair and searching as Western society reels under the blows of steadily increasing personal disorientation and societal dissolution.

What can we do as Muslims to help? First of all, we must build true Qur'ānic societies throughout the Muslim World. Without these, we cannot establish equitable and viable accommodation for the interaction of men and women in society. In addition, we cannot hope to establish in the coming generations a respect for and loyalty to our societies and their accompanying institutions if pseudo-Islamic societies are the only ones we are capable of producing and maintaining. Pseudo-Islamic measures or institutions are actually anti-Islamic; for they posit a model which cannot be respected, and attach to it the label of "Islam." In the minds of many Muslims as well as non-Muslims, this results in a wrongful transfer of the onus of the faulty institution to the religion of Islam itself.

We must educate our fellow Muslims – and especially the youth for they are the leaders of tomorrow – with regard to the importance and viability of their Qur'ānic traditions concerning women, the family and society. Despite the failure of alternative contemporary Western Social patterns, some Muslims seem to hanker after the Western brand of sexual equality, its unisex ideas, and modes of behavior, overemphasis on individualism or personal freedom from responsibility, and the nuclear family system. We must awake to the dangers which accompany such social ideas and practices. If the consequences of these ideas and practices are not pointed out and combatted, we are doomed to an unfortunate future as such social experiments are to fail ultimately.

But even this is not an adequate response for us as Muslims. As vicegerents of Allah on earth (2:30), it is our duty to be concerned about the whole world and about all of God's creatures. In the light of the command to propagate the will of Allah in every corner of the earth, we should not neglect to suggest or offer the good that we know to others. It is time for Islam and the Muslims to present their solutions of the problems of contemporary society, not only to the Muslim audience, but to the non-Muslim audience as well. This can and should be done through the living example of true Qur'ānic societies in which the problems of men and women are resolved. It should also be done through informative writings and discussions by our scholars which could be made available to Muslims and non-Muslims alike.

There is no better way to serve the will of Allah and the whole of mankind. There is no better *da'wah* than such offering of a helping hand to the struggling victims of contemporary society.

Notes

1. Allah promises the hypocrites, both men and women, and the disbelievers fire of hell for their abode. It will suffice them. Allah curses them, and theirs is lasting torment. (9:68).
2. See also 9:67-72.
3. This is a *hadīth* of the Prophet, *sallallahu alehi wasallam.* See also Muhammad 'Izzat Darwāzah, *Al-Mar'ah fī al-Qur'ān wal Sunnah* (Beirut: al-Maktabah al-'Asriyyah, 1980), p. 44, 47, 51.
4. Muhammad Fu'ad 'Abd al-Bāqi, *al-Lu'lu' wal Marjān fī mā ittafaqa fīhi al-Shaykhāni* (Beirut: Dār al-Kitāb al-Jadid, 1970), I, pp. 30-31.
5. Hajji Faysal ibn Hajji Uthmān, "Women and Nation-Building: Systematic and Contemporary Analysis of the Problem of Woman in Contemporary Malay Muslim Society (Ph.D. dissertation to be presented to Temple University), p. 85.
6. Muhammad Khayrāt, *Markaz al-mar'ah fī al-Islām* (Cairo: Dār al-Ma'ārif, 1975), p. 108.
7. Monard G. Paulsen, "Women, Legal Rights of," *Encyclopedia Americana* (Danbury, Conn.: Americana Corp., 1980), Vol. 29, pp. 108-109.
8. "...unto men a fortune from that which they have earned, and unto women a fortune from that which they have earned..." (4:32)
9. See Mustafa al-Sibā'i, *al-Mar'ah bayn al-fiqh wal qānūn* (Aleppo: Al-Maktabah al-'Arabiyyah, 1976), p. 38; Muhammad 'Izzat Darwāzah, *Al-Dustūr al-Qur'āni fī Shu'ūn al-Hayāt* (Cairo:'Isā al-Bābi al-Halabi, n.d.), p. 78.
10. "O you who believe! It is not lawful for you to inherit forcibly the women (of your deceased kinsmen) nor (that) you should put constraint upon them that you may take away a part of that which you have given them, unless they be guilty of flagrant lewdness. But consort with them in kindness, for if you hate them it may happen that you hate a thing wherein Allah has placed much good." (4:19)
11. In describing the Women's Liberation movement in America, Caroline Bird writes that, "They would abolish the notion of intrinsic differences between the nature of males and females commonly cited to validate these conventions [i.e., marriage, the family, male-female relationships, etc.]" ("Women's Liberation," *Encyclopedia Americana*, vol. 29, p. 111a).
12. In 1979 in the United States, in contrast to 2, 331,000 marriages there were, 1,181,000 divorces according to a 1983 almanac. Each year the percentage of divorces rises significantly.

Chapter IV

An Extended Family Model
from Islamic Culture

everal works already available in print have given detailed
description of the Islamic family (Abdal-Ati 1974; 1977; Esposito 1974; Ahmad 1974; Lutfiyya 1966; Fuller 1961). It is
not my intention to attempt a repetition of those works. Instead, this
paper will present, first, a summary description of the Islamic[1] family, which will facilitate our focussing attention on some characteristics of that structure which might be therapeutic for the social problems we face today in North American society. Whether we be followers of Islam, of Christianity, of Judaism or "Fitzliputzli-ism," life
in North America in the 1970s presents inordinate strains on the
family system as we know it and, as a result of this social disorganization or reorganization, often causes serious damage to individuals
as well. Second, this paper will discuss these problems and their possible solutions through some form of extended[2] family organization.
Third, it will present some prerequisites for the success of such a social plan

The *'A'ilah* of Islamic Culture

There are extended family systems operative in various cultures
and regions of the world, but the one chosen as a model for comparative study in this presentation is that of the Islamic *'ā'ilah*, as the
extended family is known in Arabic-speaking regions. My information regarding this extended family was derived, first of all, from
the two sources which have served as guide in both religious and
secular matters for the Muslim peoples for over thirteen centuries.
In the first of these, the Qur'ān, there are numerous passages which
pertain to obligations and expectations of members of a family. No
less important a source for prescriptive information on the Islamic
family is the large number of sayings noted by companions of the
Prophet Muhammad, *sallallahu alehi wasallam*, and later recorded
in the collections of hadith. Second, information was derived from

works on the family by contemporary Muslims; third, from the published results of sociological and anthropological field research; fourth, from informants and observation while I lived or visited in various Muslim countries of the Middle East, Pakistan and southeast Asia; and fifth, from my personal experience as wife, daughter-in-law, sister-in-law, and mother within a closely knit Muslim kinship organisation.

To describe the Islamic family means to describe a social institution which is recognizable over a wide geographic area. Despite some regional variations due to local customs which have been carried over from pre-Islamic social structures and institutions of the various regions, the important features of the *'ā'ilah* have relevance among Muslims living in north and central Africa, in the Middle East, in a large portion of the South Asia, in Malaysia, Indonesia, and the southern Philippine Islands.[3]

Composition

A contemporary Muslim sociologist has described the Islamic family as an organization of individuals who are "related to one another through blood ties or marital bonds and whose relatedness is such that it entails mutual role expectations..." (Abdal Ati 1974). In addition, it is necessary to add that the Islamic family is a partilineal, patrilocal network which accords little significance to the isolated nuclear family unit except among highly Westernized Muslims. In fact, there seems to be no precise term to designate the nuclear family in Arabic.[5] The Muslim extended family or *'ā'ilah* includes three or four generations of mutually dependent individuals who are commonly nucleated in a single residence or in separate but proximate accomodations. The family which shares a common residence has been designated as "residentially extended" while that whose members share the same roles and dependencies but are residentially dispersed to a greater or lesser degree is described as functionally extended (Farsoun 1670, 257) or modified extended. The *'ā'ilah* includes not only mother and father and their unwed children, but also married sons and their wives and children, in addition to unwed paternal aunts and uncles (Lutfiyya 1966: 142). It may include the various cells of polygynous marriages, which are legally and socially acceptable but statistically rare in Islamic society. When the grandfather or eldest member of the family dies, the eldest married uncle or another of the married males becomes the nucleus for a new *'ā'ilah* organization.

The individual members descendent from a common paternal ancestor also claim membership in a larger organization. This *hamūlah* or clan has its own weaker ties of dependency and responsibility which accord with the less direct blood relationship. They are evidenced in the terms *ibn 'amm* (son of paternal uncle) and *bint 'amm* (daughter of paternal uncle) by which the members address their peers, and *'amm* (paternal uncle) or *'ammah* (paternal aunt) used for all elders of the *hamūlah*. Beyond this the Individual Muslim also feels a "kinship" with all other members of the *ummah*, or the world community of Muslims. He refers to its members as *ikhwān* or "brothers" and *akhawāt* or "sisters."

Roles

It has been observed and clearly stated that in the Islamic family the roles of men and women are complementary rather than competitive (Nelson 1968:60; Saleh 1972:196), different rather than discriminatory of either sex (Ahmad 1974:15-16; Abdal-Ati 1975: 2-3). In other words, the male and female roles are described as equal in importance but not identical in substance. For the female, her role as wife and mother is considered "the most sacred and essential one" (Badawi 1975:141). There is nothing in Islam, however, to prevent her from fulfilling other roles in society if they are not undertaken at the expense of her success in her domestic obligations. As compensation for her fulfilling these female roles, strong social, moral as well as legal measures are enlisted for imposing on the male members of society the obligation to provide for, support and protect all female members of the *'ā'ilah* – wives, sisters, aunts, mothers, widows, daughters – as well as all other needy kin. The wife receives a marriage gift (*mahr*) from her husband which belongs to her exclusively, even should she be divorced later (Anderson 1970:494). It is to be divided in immediate and deferred portions, the former received by the wife at the time of marriage, the latter as a kind of "severance settlement" in case of divorce. The woman usually returns to her family of orientation in case of divorce, and her male relatives provide for her support. The former husband is responsible, however, for her maintenance during a *three-month period* (*'iddah*) following the divorce (Qur'ān 2-241), and for longer periods if she is pregnant or there are children for whom she is caring (2:233).

The *'ā'ilah* thus has not only a social function; it also acts as an economic unit for mutual aid and assistance to its members. Social and economic activities are undertaken jointly, and their benefits shared by the family jointly.[6] The only exception to this is that women who join the family through marriage retain their legal personalities, their maiden names,[7] and their right to full possession and control over their possessions, their property and its earnings (4:23).

The Islamic family system is supported by the religious writings of Islam. The importance of marriage (4:1), of having and raising children (7:189-190), of close attachment to kin (4:8; 4:36; 17:26) – all these features have religious basis in the Qur'ān itself as well as in the Sunnah or example of the Prophet Muhammad. In addition, the religious laws which have been derived from these two basic sources have given further reinforcement to the extended family system through specific provisions for inheritance and support based on nearness of relationship and sex. Different law schools (*madhāhib*) may differ on small points (e.g., amount of customary dower, minimum age of bride and groom, regulations regarding care of children in case of divorce), but the major directives evidence an overwhelming conformity. This has provided an important influence for the Islamic family to develop in a relatively uniform pattern, even though manifested over such a wide geographic area.[8]

The Extended Family and Contemporary American Society

The nuclear or conjugal family of Western society has been the object of much concern and speculation in recent times. For decades thinkers have viewed the changes in its structure and function with no little concern. The contemporary situation of the family has been designated as a "predicament," a "dilemma," a "tragedy"; and some define the disturbance as a "violent breaking up of a system" (Carle C. Zimmerman, quoted in Adams 1973:353). Others have been more optimistic, feeling that the changes are more signs of reorganization than of complete disintegration. They express the belief that the important functions the family fulfils cannot be covered by any other known social institution (Nimkoff 1965:357-62; Schelsky 1954:331-335) and therefore that the present disturbance is more a period of restructuring than collapse. It is argued that even in those societies where one or more of the functions usually ascribed to the family can be or have been taken over by other societal institutions, the residual functions cannot be satisfied by that substitute institution or institutions. For example, after the early attempts by Communist Russia and the Israeli kibbutzim to completely supplant the family in their societies, it became apparent that the family was a necessity which could not be eradicated without serious detriment to its members, and subsequently to society. It would seem therefore that we must attempt to respond to changes in our lives and in the family, helping direct the course of its future development in order to ensure its successful functioning in the future.

Some of the recent changes in the family represent reactions to such discoveries of science as artificial insemination, improvements in contraception, incubator birth and so on. Others are due to the myriad changes in social, economic, and political factors in contemporary society (e.g., urbanization, widening role of governmental agencies, increase in size and impersonal nature of productive organizations, mobility, increased employment of women, declining birth rate, overpopulation). The family has also been compelled to face drastic changes in ideas concerning the Absolute and the relation of man to religious ideas and religious institutions. Organized religion no longer exerts the stabilizing influence it formerly had on the family, and there is a profound lack of consensus on what is right and what is wrong, what is desirable and what is undesirable.

Whether these changes are seen as "dissolution" or as "progress," no one can fail to realize that there are drastic "inconsistencies" (Adams 1973:350) between the functions demanded of the contemporary American family and the adaptation of the prevalent institution to fulfil those needs. As a result of this imbalance, adults and children in our society – as well as society itself – are suffering immeasurable damage. As participants in that society, we cannot be oblivious to these problems. We have an obligation at least to try to stem the tide of "disintegration," or – if you will – to direct the course of "progress." The benefits which can be expected from the family in its role as buffer and liason organization between the individual and the larger segments of society or not being attained under the present nuclear family system prevalent in North America society. In fact, the social disorganization experienced by the middle class in the mid-1970's is nearly as great as that which characterized the low income family of the early 1960's (Woodward and Malamud 1975:48).[9] Not only is the nuclear family in its new circumstances failing to do its job; the high divorce rate[10] is truncating that family cell still further. One American child in six is now raised in a single parent family, often a parent who, because of financial necessity, is also a working parent. The fact that the remarriage rate is also high does little to alleviate the sociological and psychological harm done to the family members, and especially to the children involved.

In investigating remedies and alternatives for improving our contemporary and future American society, we need to combat the reluctance to consider the extended family as a viable solution to our societal problems or as a directive toward that goal. The extended family includes a wide set of mutual responsibilities, but it also includes a wide set of advantages and benefits. Before we reject the increased obligations as unacceptable, before we throw out any infringement on our individual freedom as intolerable, let us realize that we are today paying a tremendous price for this freedom, a societally devastating burden for our escape from responsibility. No doubt it is time for us all to look hard and long at alternatives for the future. This is true for those societies which are already deeply involved in the problems resulting from family "disintegration" or "progress," as well as for those developing societies which stand at the crossroads and are still deciding on their future direction.

The advantages that could be derived from some form of extended family system seem manifold. We shall deal here with its possible contribution to only some of our contemporary problems.

Women's Role

One of the problems facing North American society today is the indecision about women's role in the family and society. Recognizing the injustices which have been suffered by the female members of society in many places and periods, we would suggest that the proper remedy lies not in a rampant individualism which causes woman to forsake her responsibilities to husband, parents and even to children in her endeavor to be "liberated." This so-called freedom is creating instead a new kind of bondage for many women. They are being called upon to fill more than their share of the societal burden. They are being pressured to combine the role of homemaker and mother with that of a job or a career or risk the condemnation of their society. A large proportion of the female population is fulfilling a male role and a female role at the same time. In most cases, these women have failed to succeed at both. As a result of their struggle, the male members of society are also being pushed into a correlative double role – to be maintainers and wage earners at the same time as they tend the kids and cook the meals and launder the clothes. Such mixing of responsibilities, whether for the female or male, is bound to result in frustration and tragedy.

The male suffers not only physical difficulty as he attempts to take over some of the wife's obligations which she is unable to fulfil in her new multiple role as career woman-wife-mother; in such situations his intellectual and emotional satisfaction are also curtailed. His wife does not have the mental or emotional reserve energy to listen to his problems and successes. She has no time to share in his plans when she has to cope with her double set of problems, originating outside as well as inside the home.

A childless couple has less difficulty in managing such a situation, but the majority of American families have one or more children. The mad dash for jobs outside the home has seriously increased the number and severity of physical, mental, and emotional problems among young children. Children are often inadequately cared for by babysitters or day care centers; others are left to fend for themselves as "latchkey" children until the parents return from their separate jobs. Statistics leave little doubt that these children, their parents, and society are in need of drastic help. Every year at least one million children run away from home in the United States. Juvenile delinquency is increasing so rapidly that today one child in every nine can be expected to appear in juvenile court before the age of eighteen, and suicide has become the second most important cause of death among young people between the ages of fifteen and twenty-four in this country (Woodward and Malamud 1975:48). Often the strains on mother and father and children become so unbearable that the family is broken by divorce, and the problems multiply with the increased polarization between individuals. Single parents, whether male or female, experience even greater problems in coping with the multi-role life.

Such difficulties could be alleviated by an extended family system in which elder or unmarried members of the family cover some of the child-rearing burdens of the working or even the non-working mother and enable her to provide the back-up physical, intellectual, and emotional support needed by the working males. The wife would then enjoy a real "liberation" to devote her major efforts to overseeing her family responsibilities; or, if other women in the family are free and wish to fulfil that role, to pursue a career of her choice with free conscience. The extended family organization as exemplified in the *'ā'ilah* makes it possible for women to choose to have career without detriment to any individual member of the family or any sector of society.

Loneliness

A second problem in modern society is the personal loneliness experienced by many of its members. In this regard, we mention especially the older men and women who do not fit into the nuclear kinship unit. The fate of the aged is to live in isolation from intergenerational contact once their children have grown, their loneliness and isolation broken only by occasional dutiful visits from children or grandchildren. When they become unable to manage their physical affairs, they are sent to old folks' or nursing homes where they await death. Their family lives seem to end with the completion of their procreation and child-rearing functions. In the Islamic family these members of an elder generation continue to fulfil an important role in the family throughout their lives and thereby provide service for the other members of the family as well as make their own lives meaningful for the longest possible period of time. The respect accorded to elderly members of the family is not merely a matter of social convention. It is backed by Qur'ānic directives as well (17:23-24; 29:8; 31:14; 46:15-18).

The loneliness problems of the unmarried or divorced men and women in American society, the singles crowd, are hardly less crucial as the commentaries on computer dating organizations and singles commerical establishments give evidence. Their inculsion in an extended family system would provide them an honorable re-entry into societal relationships with reciprocal benefits to all members of the family organization. Whether male or female, whether wage earners or in charge of domestic or child care duties, they could play an important role in an extended family situation. The social activities of that family would prevent the loneliness produced by their exclusion in the nuclear family society.

Disintegration of Moral Fibre

A third major problem in contemporary society involves the disintegration of moral fibre. Crimes of every nature and description fill the courts and prisons of our land with culprits and infringe on the peaceful existence of a large segment of the population. Security in the cities of North America has become a dreamed of luxury known only by past generations. Even leaders of the nation are found to be lacking in the most basic features of honest behavior. There is no doubt that one of the major reasons for this steadily deteriorating situation is our failure to adequately socialize our children. An extended family system could give both men and women the choice of fulfilling themselves in a career or in the family, or in both at different periods of their life, without risking damage to their children, themselves and society by their failing to provide adequate home training for their children. No moral or intellectual training can hope to succeed which is left in the hands of the child's peer group, the schools, the street gangs, or an uncontrolled television set. No feeling of emotional security can be engendered in a child whose adult family members have no time to spend with him. The problems that such "child-rearing" generates will be far greater to parents and society than the inconvenience of less privacy and the curb on individualism that the extended family grouping entails.

It is not only a matter of proper childhood training that contributes to the disintegration of moral fibre. Just as damaging is the mobility and anonymity of our society. Neighborhoods have broken up. Job opportunities propel both men and women from one end of the country to another. Even living within one urban area all one's life can fail to give an individual a feeling of belonging, because of the rapid turnover in neighbourhood populations, the consolidated school systems, and the dispersal of citizens for higher education and job opportunities. The individual is forever the stranger among strangers, feeling no pull to conform to the moral and social expectations of old friends and relatives. No one knows him, nor he is freed of moral compunctions regarding his deeds and thoughts. The reintegration of such adults into an extended family organization which is mindful of his moral as well as physical welfare could provide great benefit to society as well as to its individual members.

The Parent Problem

A fourth problem which confronts society today is the difficulty of parenting our children. According to John Anderson, a director for the Family Services of Detroit and a father himself, "Parents have lost control of their families. They feel inadequate, overwhelmed – I know I do" (quoted by Woodward and Malamud 1975:48). The example of the *'a'ilah* offers several remedies for the parenting problems with which so many couples or single parents are confronted today. One of these derives from the fact that the greater the number of adults available in the home, the more a child has opportunity to spend his time with and be influenced by them rather than by uncertain influences, television, or his peer group. It is for this reason that the extended family which has a single residential nucleus usually provides much more effective parenting than the extended family which is residentially dispersed, though still bound by commitments of obligation and service.

Second, disciplinary problems with children will in fact be far less frequent and severe if the child knows the parent is backed by aunts, uncles, and or grandparents who are "on-the-scene" to enforce any adult decision. The sheer force of numbers among the adults will in fact be a stabilizing element on juvenile caprice which no husband-wife team or single parent has at his disposal.

Third, the conflict which can sometimes mar the relationship between one adult and a particular child in a nuclear family situation is alleviated when that parent is only one of many adults in the family. In such a circumstance the child can relate to another adult of the same sex as the parent with whom he has difficulty, and in that way avoid any of the psychological problems that might accrue from a similar estrangement in a nuclear family situation.

Fourth, the generation gap which often hampers parenting could be alleviated by an extended family system. There has always been some difference in the thinking of members of different generations. It is quite natural that one views events, actions, and ideas in one way at age ten, in another way at age twenty, and at still another way at the age of fifty. The experience of years has a telling effect on any individual. That is not something that any society can hope to change or even wants to remedy. It is even a desirable phenomenon. A generation gap of the late twentieth century, however, has become a problem which causes a serious loss of advisory and educative help to the younger members of society and a devastating loss of assistance and companionship for its older members. By growing in a socializing atmosphere which provides close contact with members of at least three generations, the children of an extended family similar to the *'ā'ilah* would be much less likely to reject offhand the influence of the elders of the family. The constant presence of some member of another generation would keep every child aware of the wide range of interests and ideas in our multi-generation world and thus give him a better training for his future life. In addition, it would keep the older members of society "young" through constant contact with the junior members.

Prerequisites for the Success of the Extended Family in North American Society

Even from such a brief perusal of problems relating to the family which are faced by contemporary society, it is evident that the extended family has many advantages to offer. However, its implementation requires more than the mere realization of its worth by a few social reformers or social planners. It has prerequisites for success which are suggested by the Islamic example.

Propaganda Campaign

One of these prerequisites is a propaganda campaign to counter the heritage of ill will with which the extended family and the interdependence it demands are viewed. In North America many of our contemporaries consider any infringement on individualism and independence as wrong. They fail to realise that it is precisely to the extent that they are dependent on others and others are dependent on them that their psychological well-being and their adjustment in society – in fact, their sanity – depends. A campaign is needed to convince people that even values such as individual freedom are subject to misuse and overemphasis. We must break down the "reluctance to see that the excessive emphasis upon the isolated individual is the tragedy of modern man, leading inevitably to the dissolution of family unity and family integrity" (Anshen 1959:11).

Upgrading of Domestic Roles

Second, there is a need for a drastic change in the grading and treatment of domestic roles. Whereas Islamic society views motherhood as the most prestigious role of woman, the liberationists have so downgraded and repudiated the household, the child-bearing and child-rearing roles that no woman feels any longer able to hold her head aloft if she does not have another occupation outside the home – however menial or less beneficial to society, to herself, and her family that occupation may be. We have been brainwashed into thinking that only the factory job, the secretarial post, the teaching or executive position demands intelligence, perseverance, and skill. How mistaken we are! And how much our families and all their members are suffering for this blindness! It should be one of our most important lessons for the coming generations that the job of homemaker is one which demands as much intelligence, perseverance and skill as any job outside the home. We must never underestimate the importance of the domestic roles which mold tomorow's citizenry at the same time; as they maintain today's society. It is time we stopped telling the lazy girl student that she will be good for only cooking or caring for children if she does not improve in her studies. Instead we should give homemaker's and mother's medals! – not just for being a homemaker or for being a biological mother, but for being an exemplary homemaker or mother. If we restore to these roles the importance they deserve, we would fulfil one of the prerequisites of the success of an extended family system and at the same time widen the options for both male and female members of our society.

Decentralization

Another way of ensuring the success of the extended family would be to encourage decentralization in national planning. The goal should be to provide each community with the educational, the economic, and the leisure facilities which would make it possible for young people to stay in their own communities and in their family groups at the end of their secondary schooling. The examples of poor, or of utter lack of, planning in such matters can be seen throughout the world. They can be found in many of the developing nations where "planned economies" are supposed to exist and national governments wield a powerful hand in local affairs. Industry, facilities for higher education, and recreational possibilities are often concentrated in a single center of these countries, while the rest of the nation is devoid of all such opportunities. It is true that the cities of Islamic countries seem to be more conglomerations of villages than cities in the Western sense (see Abu-Lughod 1970:664-678); yet, the separation from the residual family of the village is not a thing to be encouraged. Countries like Egypt, Pakistan and Turkey not only suffer a brain drain to Western countries; they even suffer a brain drain from countryside and village to Cairo, Karachi and Ankara. A provincial leader from the Island of Mindanao in the Philippines remarked that the local village community from which he comes is no longer encouraged to finance students to go to Manila for higher education – not to speak of sending them to America. Once outside the confines of the village, with its dearth of job, education and recreation opportunities, the young men and women are reluctant to return to sever their communities which need them so desperately.

In our own country, where organization of productive and consumptive facilities receives less direction from the government than it does in many other nations, one would not expect to find the imbalance of opportunities remedied. Actually, we are all well aware of the discrepancies in opportunities that helped clog the cities and depopulate the countryside of North America. If each community could share a measure of the nation's facilities for education, employment and recreation, there would be little need for the enforced mobility which plagues our society today and will be the disease of all developing countries tomorrow if they do not learn from our experience. Unless we can provide a stability to families and communities, we risk the dangers of continuing in a situation which has been compared to the ills suffered by a nomadic population or the families of migrant farm workers (Woodward and Malamud 1975:53;

see also Zimmerman 1947 and Sorokin 1941).

It might be argued that such decentralization involves tremendous amounts of money in relocation and industrial transportation costs. But the cost in human suffering and the irreparable damage to society which the concentration in a few major cities has brought are much more costly – costly in human life and well-being, and also costly in dollars and cents. Each year millions are spent on crime detection, on public welfare and on incarcerating deviant citizens, in addition to the money spent repairing the damage to our ecological resources which results from these overconcentrations of population.

Legal Benefits

A fourth way of encouraging the implementation of an extended family system in order to alleviate some of our contemporary social problems would be to provide legal benefits for those who support such a family system. Tax laws could be enacted which would encourage members of an extended family to maintain their needy kin regardless of age. Islamic family laws of inheritance and maintenance have played an important role in the structure and function of the family in Muslim society. New legislation in North America might include such features as tax concessions for families supporting three or more generations, inheritance laws providing not only for wife and children but for other members of the extended family as well, and provisions making well-off members of a family legally responsible for the welfare of its needy kin.

Housing

Housing requisites for the larger families would be different from those of the nuclear family, but this requirement is one that is perhaps most easy to fulfil, just as the larger homes of the last century, which accommodated the larger families prevalent at that time, were divided into small appartments, they could be expanded by the addition of rooms and removal of partitions to expand interiors.

Conclusion

North American society faces social problems in the latter half of the twentieth century which make constructive thinking on the part of social planners imperative. It is no longer prudent for the social scientist to restrict himself to the presentation of descriptive research. He must assume a constructive role in social planning if he is to avoid the accusation of irrelevance, or the worse condemnation of being unconcerned about his society, about his fellowman. In this article, cross-cultural research on the extended family as operative among the Muslim peoples is taken as a model for features of possible change that might alleviate the difficulties faced by contemporary American society.

In an opening section, the *'a'ilah* is defined by describing its composition and the contrasting roles of its male and female members. A second section enumerates some of the problems facing contemporary society in North America – the definition of women's role in society, loneliness, the deterioration of moral standards, and the parenting or socialization of children – and shows how these problems could be alleviated by adoption of some form of extended family system. A third section describes five constructive steps for bringing such a family into being in North America. The first of these is a propaganda compaign to counter the heritage of ill will with which the extended family and the interdependence it demands are viewed. Second, there is need for a drastic upgrading of the household, child-bearing and child rearing roles which have been repudiated and scorned by the women's liberation movement in their attempt to counter past injustices. The third prerequisite is for a national effort to decentralize economic, educational, and recreational opportunities throughout the country so that families need not be broken by the rush to large urban centers. A fourth way of encourageing implementation of an extended family system is through the institution of legal benefits. Possible tax, inheritance and maintenance laws are suggested. Housing requirements to correspond to altered residential patterns are the fifth prerequisite to be fulfilled.

References

Hammudah 'Abdal-'Ati, "Modern Problems, Classical Solutions: An Islamic Perspective on the Family," *Journal of Comparative Family Studies* (1974) 5 (2): 37-54.
"Women in Islam," (1975) unpublished paper.
The Family Structure in Islam: Explorations in Historicocultural Sociology (Indianapolis: American Trust Publications, 1977).

Janet Abu-Lughod, "Migrant Adjustment to City Life: The Egyptian Case," *Readings in Arab Middle Eastern Societies and Cultures*, ed. Abdulla M. Lutfiyya and Charles W. Churchill. (The Hague, Paris: Mouton, 1970), 664-678.

Bert N. Adams, *The American Family: A Sociological Interpretation*. (Chicago: Markham Publishing Co., first pub. 1971.

Khurshid Ahmad, *Family Life in Islam*. (Leicester: The Islamic Foundation, 1974).

J.N.D. Anderson, "The Eclipse of the Patriarchal Family in Contemporary Islamic Law," *Family Law in Asia and Africa*. ed. J.N.D. Anderson (New York: Frederick A. Praeger, first pub. 1967), 221-234.
"The Islamic Law of Marriage and Divorce," *Readings in Arab Middle Eastern Societies and Cultures* ed. Abdulla M. Lutfiyya and Charles W. Churchill. (The Hague, Paris: Mouton, 1970), 492-504.

Ruth Nanda Anshen, "The Family in Transition," *The Family: Its Function and Destiny*, ed. Ruth Nanda Anshen (New York: Harper and Row, 3-19, first pub. 1949).

Gamal A. Badawy, "Woman in Islam," *Islam: Its Meaning and Message*, Khurshid Ahmad (London: Islamic Council of Europe, 1975), 131-145.

Dorothy R. Blitsten, *The World of the Family* (New York: Random House, 1963).

John F. Cuber, "Alternate Models from the Perspective of Sociology," *The Family in Search of a Future: Alternate Models for Moderns*, ed. Herbert A. Otto (New York: Appleton-Century-Crofts, 1970).

John L. Esposito, "Muslim Family Law in Egypt and Pakistan: A Critical Analysis of Legal Reform, its Sources and Methodological Problems," Ph.D. dissertation, Temple University, Department of Religion (January, 1974).

Hani Fakhouri, *Kafr El Elow: An Egyptian Village in Transition* (New York: Holt, Rinehart and Winston, Inc., 1972).

S.K. Farsoun, "Family Structure and Society in Modern Lebanon," *Peoples and Cultures of the Middle East*, ed. Louise E. Sweet (Garden City: Natural History Press, 1970).

Anne H. Fuller, *Buarij: Portrait of a Lebanese Muslim Village* (Cambridge, Massachusetts: Harvard University Press, 1961).
"The World of Kin," *Readings in Arab Middle Eastern Societies and Cultures*, ed. Abdulla M. Lutfiyya and Charles W. Churchill (The Hague, Paris: Mouton, 1970), 526-534.

Paul H. Glasser, and Lois N. Glasser, ed., *Families in Crisis* (New York: Harper and Row, 1970).

William J. Goode, *World Revolution and Family Patterns* (New York: Free Press 1963).

Arthur Jeffery, "The Family in Islam," *The Family: Its Function and Destiny*, ed Ruth Nanda Anshen (New York: Harper and Row, 1959), 201-238.

Abdulla M. Lutfiyya, *Baytin: A Jordanian Village* (The Hague: Mouton and Co. 1966).

George P. Murdock, *Social Structure* (New York: Macmillan, 1949).

Cynthia Nelson, "Changing Roles of Men and Women: Illustrations from Egypt," *Anthropological Quarterly*, 1968, 41 (2):57-77.

Myer Nimkoff, ed., *Comparative Family Systems* (Boston: Houghton Mifflin, 1965).

Talcott Parsons, "The Kinship System of the Contemporary United States," *American Anthropologist*, 1943, 45:22-38.
"The Normal American Family," *Man and Civilization: The Family's Search for Survival*, Seymour M. Farber. Piero Mustacchi, and Roger H.L. Wilson, eds. (New York: McGraw-Hill, 1965).

Raphael Patai, *Golden River to Golden Road* (Philadelphia: University of Pennsylvania Press, first pub. 1962).

Edwin Terry Prothro and Lutfy Najib Diab, *Changing Family Patterns in the Arab East* (Beirut: American University of Beirut, 1974).

Paul J. Reiss, "The Extended Kinship System: Correlates of and Attitudes on Frequency of Interaction," *Marriage and Family Living*, 1962, 24:333-339.

Saneya Saleh, "Women in Islam: Their Status in Religious and Traditional Culture," *International Journal of Sociology of the Family*, 1972, 2 (2):193-201.

Helmut Schelsky, "The Family in Germany," *Marriage and Family Living*, 1954, 16:331-335.

P.A. Sorokin, *Social and Cultural Dynamics* (New York: American Book Company, 1941), four volumes.

Marvin Sussman, "The Isolated Nuclear Family: Fact or Fiction?" *Social Problems*, 1959, 6:333-340.

Kenneth L. Woodward, and Phyllis Malamud, "The Parent Gap," *Newsweek*, September, 1975, 22:48-56.

C.C. Zimmerman, *The Family and Civilization* (New York: Harper and Row, Publishers, n.d.).

Chapter V

Marriage in Islam

In order to explain how marriage is regarded and manifested in Islamic society, an organization of four major divisions has been utilized here. The first discusses general characteristics and purposes of Islamic marriage; a second outlines the specific requirements which legitimize marriage; and a third details the mechanisms for its dissolution. A fourth and final section discusses briefly the issue of change and the future.

General Characteristics of Marriage in Islam

Religion as Dominant Factor: Probably the most dominant factor that influences or has influenced Islamic marriage is religion. This is due in part to the Islamic idea that religion (*dīn*) is not a body of ideas and practices which should be practiced or which should influence only that part of human life generally designated as dealing with the sacred. In Islamic culture there is little or no conception of a bifurcation between that which is sacred and that which is secular. Instead, since every aspect of life is the creation of Allāh, it carries religious significance. It is the material with which humanity works to fulfill the will of God on earth, the ultimate human purpose in creation. Thus, for the Muslim, the ritual prayer conducted in any clean place is as equally valid and acceptable as that performed in the mosque; the commitment to political and social awareness and activity is as much a religious duty as the recitation of prayers; economic pursuits are equally regulated in accordance with religio-ethical pronouncements as the *zakāh* (Islamic levy for social welfare) and the *hajj* (pilgrimage to Makkah). Aesthetic products present not art for art's sake, but art for religion's sake: they are restatements and reminders of religious truth. In fact, every aspect of Islamic life is permeated with the effects of Qur'ānic and religious teachings. Marriage is no less affected.

In Islamic society, however, marriage is not a religious sacrament. In other words, it is not a ceremony which necessitates the involvement of any clergy, presupposes a numinous or divine involvement, or, as a consequence, tends to be regarded as an indissoluble commitment.[1] In Islam there are no priests and little notion of sacredness in marriage which surpasses that of any other similarly recommended institution of the culture. Consequently, the religion has delineated accepted procedures for its dissolution.

Although marriage is not regarded as a religious sacrament, Islam recommends it fory every Muslim. Commendations are to be found for it in the Qur'ān (4:1, 29; 7:107; 13:38; 24:32-33; 30:20), and the *hadīth* literature contains numerous passages in which celibacy is discouraged and marriage encouraged. For example, "Marriage is of my ways," the Prophet is reported to have taught, as well as, "whoever is able to marry, should marry."[2] Such stimulus from religious teachings has made marriage the goal of every Muslim and caused a considerable amount of social pressure to achieve that end for every member of the society.[3] Parents, relatives, and friends all feel committed to assist actively in the process, and few are the individuals who "escape the system."

Religion also guarantees certain rights and imposes certain responsibilities on the participants in marriage. Both men and women are regarded as deriving substantial benefits from the institution of marriage, but they are also bound to its obligations by actual Qur'ānic prescriptives and by the legal elaboration and interpretation of the scriptural passages.[4] The religious laws of personal status are therefore crucial to any understanding of Islamic marriage. It is in these laws that the most detailed enunciation of both the woman's and the man's rights and obligations is to be found. Complying with the fulfillment of those mutual responsibilities is therefore regarded as a religious obligation for both parties. The acquiescence or the failure to comply is regarded as an act carrying divine reward or punishment, and therefore it is not a matter to be taken lightly.

Also important is the fact that matrimony in Islam is as much a joining of two families as it is a joining of two individuals. Given the level of interdependence in the Islamic family, Muslims are especially likely to believe marriage necessitates a consideration of the welfare of the familial groups involved rather than merely the desires of the two individuals. For this reason a much larger participation in the choice of marriage partners is regarded as proper and beneficial than would be acceptable in a contemporary Western environment. Even after the marriage, the extended family organization reduces dependence on the single adult relationship of husband and wife and stimulates equally strong relationships between the wife or husband and other members of the family. Despite this heavily "familial" character of the Islamic marriage, the woman maintains her separate legal identity after marriage, her maiden name, her adherence to a particular school of law, and her right to separate ownership of her money, property, or financial holdings.

The Purposes of Marriage: The importance of marriage in Islamic society and its advocacy by the religious teachings rest on the avowed purposes it serves. First, Muslims regard marriage as providing a balance between individualistic needs and the welfare of the group to which the individual belongs. As such, it is regarded as a social and psychological necessity for every member of the community.

Second, marriage is a mechanism for the moral and mutually beneficial control of sexual behavior and procreation. Islam regards sexual activity as an important and perfectly healthy drive of both males and females. Thus, it is not shameful and should not be denied to members of either sex. Lack of sexual satisfaction is believed to cause personality maladjustments and to "endanger the mental health and efficiency of the society."[5] Islam, therefore, commends sex as natural and good but restricts it to participants of a union which insures responsibility for its consequences.[6]

A third purpose of marriage is its provision of a stable atmosphere for the rearing of children. Islam sees this purpose as inextricably tied to an extended family system. The extended family may vary in size, even in residential proximity, as is evidenced in different regions of the Muslim world, but the cohesion of its members is inextricably bound to Qur'ānic prescriptions and Islamic law. These explicitly enunciate the rights and obligations of its members and the legal extent of those benefits and responsibilities.[7]

Fourth, marriage assures crucial economic benefits for women during their child-bearing years. Self-support during this period is difficult, if not impossible, for mothers who have no outside help. Even if sustained by the "supermom," of which we hear so much in recent times, the physical and emotional toll on such persons is beyond what most individuals can tolerate.

Fifth, the close companionship of the marital partners provides emotional gratification for both men and women. The importance of this purpose of marriage in Islam is evidenced by repeated references in the Qur'ān and *hadīth* literature to the quiescence (30:21; 7:189) and protective nature (9:71) of the bond between the husband and wife. The man and woman are considered to be so close that they are described as garments of one another (2:187). The kindness, love, and consideration enjoined on the partners appear repeatedly in both religious and legal texts.

Specific Requirements for Marriage in Islam

Given its general characteristics and purposes as outlined above, Islamic marriage also entails certain specific features which are regarded necessary for its legitimacy. Let us first specify the criteria which must be met by the participants themselves.

Limitation of Participants: Applying to both parties are the Islamic boundaries of incestuous union. The list of acceptable persons whom one can marry rests on a firm ground of conformity since the basic exogamy or endogamy[8] patterns are fixed by the Qur'ān and hadīth.[9] Islam prescribes limits on marriages between certain blood (consanguine) relatives, between others closely related through marriage (affinal relatives), and between lactational relatives – that is, those who have been nursed by the same woman.[10] Since the institution of the wet nurse and the reciprocal nursing of their babies by women with close familial or affinal ties have often been widespread, the lactational limits have proved very influential for discouraging inbreeding. The jurists of the different schools have unanimously adhered to that prohibition and accepted the authenticity of the hadīth on this matter,[12] although the details of how much nursing and how much milk constitutes a prohibiting amount, the ages of affected children, and so forth, were sometimes disputed.

The definition of allowable marriage partners is considered by Muslims to fulfill two major purposes: to prevent the biological effects of inbreeding, and to guard against excessive familiarity between sexual partners. Such familiarity is regarded as cause for sexual indifference in the partners. Therefore, marriage with someone as close as a mother, sister, daughter, or aunt would result, in most cases, in a denial of sexual gratification for the marriage partners. In the Muslim village, young people of the opposite sex are separated from the age of puberty or before. If they are to realize a sexually successful marriage in the village, the possibilities for familiarity must be limited and the aura of mystery and excitement engendered by marriage candidates of the opposite sex preserved. Whether consciously or unconsciously pursued by the Muslim peoples, this concern seems to be at the base of the preference – or, in some parts of the Muslim world, the demand – for segregation of the sexes. That is a much more logical underlying purpose for segregation than the need to curb sexual promiscuity. The latter is almost an impossibility in the close quarters and intensive interaction of the village.[12]

There are also religious affiliation boundaries for participation in an Islamic marriage. The male must be a Muslim; the female may be a Muslim, Jew, or Christian (5:6). Sometimes the religious requirements for the female have been interpreted more widely to include anyone who is not idolatrous. The prohibition against a non-Muslim man's marrying a Muslim woman is, however, Qur'ānic and has been unequivocally adhered to by all the legal schools.

Though a few early jurists rejected completely the idea of intermarriage, most Muslims have considered it permissible under certain conditions.[13] The Qur'ānic and legal directives on intermarriage tended to be reinforced by the circumstances of the early centuries of Islamic history. As traders, warriors, missionaries, teachers, administrators, and religious or education-seeking pilgrims, many Muslim men traveled to live in different parts of the world. They often lived in predominantly non-Muslim societies where Muslim women were not available for marriage partners. Women, on the other hand, tended to remain in their predominantly Muslim societies and therefore had access to Muslim male partners.

There were no age limitations for marriage partners in Islamic culture until recent times. Since the individuals remained part of a larger family structure which did not call upon them to support themselves, to set up their own home, or to cope unaided with the problems of parenting children, Islam held a much more relaxed view of the prior preparedness for marriage. As the extended family of certain urban environments has been weakened in recent times, a greater emphasis has been placed on the readiness of the married couple to live a more isolated and self-sufficient existence. This has stimulated an appeal by certain individuals and groups in a number of Muslim countries to call for the setting of minimum age limits for marriage.[14] Since marriage in Islam means the signing of a contract, with consummation following perhaps at a much later time, marriage of minors did not raise the same sort of problems it might in another societal complex. This does not mean that the custom of child marriage was never abused; it does mean that this Islamic custom need not be detrimental if practiced in tandem with a properly functioning Islamic society. Not its use but its misuse in an Islamically inconsistent social complex has generated Muslim concern and the recent need for a minimum-age limitation for marriage partners.

Some writers have attributed the recent calls for minimum-age requirements to Western influences on Islamic thinking and customs. In fact, that argument has been the main thrust of conservative opposition to the initiation of age restrictions on marriage. It seems much more likely that this so-called "Westernization" would not have taken root unless the misuse or imbalance within the system had not made some sort of change necessary.

Another requirement which relates to the qualifications of the marriage participants is that the Muslim woman must be unmarried. If she has formerly been married, she should not be pregnant or in the first three months following her previous marriage, a period known as *'iddah*, in which she may not be aware of a possible pregnancy. The former husband is obliged to support her during the *'iddah* or until the birth of her child, after which she may remarry. Such restrictions help verify paternity of a child resulting from the earlier marriage.

The male partner in marriage, however, is not limited to a single marriage. Islam can be described as permitting polygynous marriage, that is, it is a society in which plural marriages for males are possible. In Islamic society, however, only a small portion of the males practice polygyny. If those that do are known to have no valid reason for taking another wife,[15] or do not treat their wives with the complete equality commanded by the Qur'ān (4:3; 129), Muslims judge such instantiation of this form of marriage as un-Islamic and religiously and morally reprehensible. As an excuse for sexual promiscuity, the practice is unconditionally condemned, but, if practiced according to Islamic moral exhortations and legal provisions, Muslims regard polygyny as a more equitable and humane solution to certain situations than the unconditional demand for monogamy.[16] In some schools of law, a woman who wishes to prevent her husband's future second marriage can ask that such a stipulation be written into the marriage agreement.

Mechanistic Requirements

Other specific requirements of Islamic marriage pertain to the actual execution of the marriage rather than to the qualities of its participants. These are designated here as "mechanistic requirements."

A Written Contract: Marriage in Islam constitutes an agreement between a man and a woman which is embodied in a written contract. The marriage agreement includes specification of the dower (both an initial and delayed portion, see section on dower), signatures of the two participants and of their respective witnesses, and other terms agreed upon by the parties concerned. The contract is a legal document, which is filed with the local Islamic registry of the government and upholdable in a court of law.

The occasion for the signing of the contract is called *'aqd nikāh* ("marriage contract"). It usually takes place at the home of the bride's parents, in the presence of members of the family and close friends. The *'aqd nikāh* is accompanied by the surrender of the agreed-upon initial dower and the exchange of gifts by the marriage partners. It also marks the beginning of preparations for the consummation of the marriage. The actual marriage requirements are fulfilled in the *'aqd nikāh*, and the marriage is complete, but it is not until the *'urs* or actual wedding party that the marriage is consummated and the bride moves to the home of her husband. This may take place shortly after the contract signing or at a much later time, as the parties desire.

The *'urs* may be a simple party or an elaborate occasion. Refreshments, activities, and entertainment vary according to tastes, financial capabilities, and regional preferences. It may take place at the groom's home or at a public place reserved for the occasion. It is the common practice not only for gifts to be presented to the bride and groom by guests on this occasion but also for the couple to reciprocate with a token of their gratitude – usually a small dish or platter for carrying sweets or an item of clothing for closer relatives. These vary in extravagance to match the economic situation of the wedding participants.

The clothing of the bride and groom varies from one level of society to another and from one region to another. In the Arab mashriq (near the eastern end of the Mediterranian Sea), for example, the wedding dress may be a white gown and headcovering similar to that common in Western societies or an elaborate example of the local style. Men wear Western-style suits or traditional dress. In Pakistan, brides are clothed in crimson shalwār-qamīs or gharara suit elaborately decorated with gold, while grooms don the traditional sherwāni with its high collar and buttoned front. In Malaysia the typical attire for both bride and groom is a traditionally styled outfit made of the locally produced brocade woven with gold threads. If the wedding couple come from wealthy families, the clothing may be so heavily decorated with the precious metal that the pair have difficulty in moving. But this does not present too much of a problem since the function of the *'urs* is an elaborate reception at which the bride and groom and their families accept the congratulations and best wishes of friends and relatives.

Two Adult Witnesses: Two witnesses – one representing the bride, the other representing the groom – are a necessary feature of the marriage-contract signing. Where possible, these are the two fathers of the couple, but any other adult Muslim could legitimately fill this role. No other intermediary is required for the performance of a marriage. Any person who is chosen by the parties may make and accept the marriage proposal. Often, however, a *qādi* or Muslim lawyer attends as a registrar of the marriage.

***Su'āl* and *Ijāb*: ("Question and Consent"):** Another element of a legitimate marriage in Islamic society is an explicit request by the groom and his family or representatives and an explicit consent to marriage by the bride and her family or representatives, which may be either in writing or oral. The Qur'ān does not deal specifically with this matter, but there are a number of instances from the *hadīth* literature which pertain to this question.[17] The story is told of a woman in the time of Muhammad who demanded and was accorded by the Prophet the right to repudiate her marriage because she had not been asked and therefore had not given her consent to the bond.[18] Despite strongly authenticated instances in the *sunnah* ("example") of the Prophet Muhammad, Muslim jurists have varied in their interpretations of the guardian's powers in arranging marriage for his wards or children. Some deem it a necessary condition for the father to seek the consent of his daughter before he gives her in marriage. Others argue that it is commendable rather than necessary. Still others limit the need for the consent of the bride to the mature woman who is a widow or divorcee.[19]

Dower: A fourth requirement of the Islamic marriage is a marriage gift or dower to the bride by the groom. This gift may consist of anything deemed suitable by the participants – money, real estate, or other valuable items. In some cases it has entailed the transfer of great wealth to the bride; in others, it has been as modest as an iron ring or a token coin.[20] No maximum has been set by Islamic law, though some schools have specified minimums.[21] Such details are worked out by the representatives of the bride and groom prior to the *'aqd nikāh* and are specified in the written contract.

The dower may be immediate – that is, given at the time of signing the *'aqd nikāh*. More often, the parties agree that the dower be divided into two parts: one portion (the *mahr*) surrendered to the bride at the time of marriage, and another delayed portion (the *mu'akhkhar*) which falls due in case of death or divorce. If a man dies, Islamic law provides that his widow's *mu'akhkhar* settlement be paid before any other commitment on his estate is honore.

The immediate dower may be used for the trousseau and the household purchases needed for the newly married couple. At other times it is a kind of economic insurance for the future welfare of the bride, in which case she invests it and draws benefits from it. In the case of poor people, the amounts are so negligible that they can be viewed as little more than a symbol of the groom's willingness to take on financial responsibility for his future wife. Amounts of dower vary not only with the difference in the economic capabilities of different grooms and their families but also according to regional practices and social levels within a particular society.

It is clear that the Islamic marriage is not a "ceremony." Although it may be associated with a number of elaborate activities (procession of the bride to her new husband's home, beautification of the bride prior to marriage with henna decorations, gift-giving and well wishing of friends and relatives, elaborate clothing, refreshments, and entertainment), marriage in Islam is essentially a legal agreement between two individuals and two families. While carrying the sanction and blessing of the religion, it cannot be considered a sacred ceremony. Marriage, like so many other aspects of Islamic culture, is neither wholly sacred nor wholly secular, neither religious nor nonreligious.

Dissolution of Marriage

Death

Dissolution of marriage occurs either by death of one of the parties or by divorce. In the case of the woman's death, there are inheritance laws which pertain to her wealth since her property remains separate from that of her husband. There are similarly specific requirements for the distribution of his wealth following the death of the husband. Other requirements pertain to the female survivor. These include payment of the *mu'akhkhar* dower to the widow and the illegality of the widow's remarriage before completion of the three month *'iddah* period in which the possibility of pregnancy can be determined. During this time, the widow is financially supported by her late husband's estate. If she is pregnant, maintenance is guaranteed until birth of the child or the end of the nursing period, but she must not remarry until the birth of her child.

Divorce

More complicated is the dissolution of marriage through legal divorce. Although it is generally believed that dissolution of marriage takes place in Islam only by male repudiation of the wife – that is, by his pronouncing three times, "I divorce you" – the fact is that Islamic law provides various mechanisms and channels for ending a marriage. Despite the variety of means for divorce, it has remained a repugnant act in Islamic society,[22] to be invoked only when all methods of reconciliation have been exhausted. Some types of divorce are male-instigated, others female-instigated; still others are the result of mutual agreement or judicial process.

Male-instigated Divorce: The most common form of divorce initiated by Muslim males is known as *talāq* ("letting go free"), which involves a series of three statements by the husband that he divorces his wife. Contrary to common opinion, these repudiation statements cannot legally be rendered at a single time. In fact, very strict rules have been established in Islamic law to prevent misuse.[23] Unfortunately, these laws have not always been enforced.

Talāq is to be pronounced with specific terms before two qualified witnesses. Each pronouncement must be made at a time when the wife is not incapacitated for sexual activity by menstrual flow. Having made the first statement of divorce, the man must wait to make the second statement until the woman completes her next monthly period. The third pronouncement must be similarly spaced. Only after the third repudiation is the divorce considered final. Each of the other two statements is revocable. The wife continues to live in her home, and she is provided full maintenance throughout the divorce proceedings. During this time, attempts are made to achieve reconciliation through the counseling and arbitration of family and friends. Only if this is not possible is the final pronouncement made and the marriage considered irrevocably broken. From that point, husband and wife are forbidden to live together or to remarry each other unless the woman has remarried someone else from whom she becomes widowed or divorced. Any Islamic divorce, like the dissolution of marriage by death, requires a three-months' waiting period in order to determine whether the divorcee is pregnant. She is not free to remarry until that period is completed or, in case of pregnancy, until she gives birth. As in the case of dissolution of marriage by death, maintenance of the wife is incumbent upon the husband for the *'iddah* and period of child-bearing.

Any *talāq* divorce not made in accordance with these rules is considered to be an aberration, or *bid'ah*. Such practice is regarded as sinful, but unfortunately the actions of some Muslims and the positions of certain jurists have not always accorded with the ideal.[24]

Female-Instigated Divorce: In Islam equitable does not mean equivalence or identity. Therefore, there are different procedures which apply to women in their initiation of divorce proceedings. The wife is entitled to originate dissolution of her marriage under four circumstances.

First, in a delegated divorce, the right of *talāq* or repudiation, by the wife may be agreed upon prior to marriage and stipulated as a condition of the marriage contract.[25] Second is a conditional divorce, a stipulation in the marriage contract that the wife will be free to ask her husband to divorce her if he does certain things contrary to his pre-marriage promises. This type of divorce is accepted by some jurists but rejected by others.[26] Third is a court divorce, in which freedom from the marriage bond is granted to a woman for any of the inadequacies of the husband which are generally regarded as legitimate causes for divorce: long absence or desertion, impotence, failure to provide adequate support, physical or mental mistreatment, serious physical or mental illness, apostasy, and proved debauchery. As noted earlier, a wife may also be granted a divorce if, upon reaching maturity, she rejects a marriage contracted by a guardian on her behalf while she was still a child. A fourth type of divorce instigated by the wife is known as *khul'*. It involves a release of the wife from the marriage contract on her agreement to pay compensation to the husband.

Mutual Consent or Mubāra'ah: When a husband and wife reach mutual agreement to dissolve their marriage, it is called *mubāra'ah*.

It differs from the *khul'* in being effected by mutual desire on the part of the marriage partners.[27]

Judicial Process: *Li'ān* or "double testimony" is the dissolution of marriage which results from the husband's accusation that his wife has committed adultery. If he proves his case (four eye-witnesses are necessary in Islamic law!), it is considered valid reason for divorce. If he has no witnesses other than himself, he must swear by God four times that his statement is true. The wife is called upon to admit her guilt or to testify in a similar way that her husband has lied about her. Both also invoke divine curses for false swearing. If no further proof either for or against the accusation can be substantiated, reconciliation between the two parties is deemed impossible, and the marriage is dissolved by judicial process.[28] Certain types of divorce instigated by women are also dealt with by the Islamic courts (see "court divorce".

Change and the Future

An increase in the number of women in the work force, increased education for women and men, the development of Islamic awareness and identity among Muslims in all parts of the world, increased mobility, concentration of populations in urban centers, increased contact with alien cultures, as well as many other contemporary facts of life may require certain adjustments in marriage practice in any society. Whether such adjustments will prove disastrous to the institution of Islamic marriage as it is now known – and, therefore, to Muslim society – or merely productive of a new synthesis of twentieth and twenty-first-century influences with the core premises depends on the ability of society to react with a strong and intelligent social conscience. Social change as such need not be unduly disruptive of Islamic marriage practices. In fact, the magnitude of the Muslim identity (nearly 1,000,000,000 persons) and the diversity of geograpic, ethnic, linguistic, and cultural backgrounds out of which these people moved toward Islamization have resulted in an extremely rich and varied tradition in marriage as in all other aspects of the civilization.

Islam has been particularly tolerant of its new converts, and those converts have been particularly ingenious in adapting their local customs to basic Islamic premises wherever possible. At the same time, there were basic premises of the faith as expressed in the Qur'ān and exemplified in the teachings and example of the Prophet Muhammad which provided a religio-cultural core with which the more superficial variations could be sympathetically related. History has confirmed that, along with a maintenance of the core, Islamic society has been flexible enough to allow regional variations as well as changes accompanying the passage of time and the variation of circumstances. Each period has had to make its "peace" with those variations of circumstances, to take that which was acceptable to the Islamic core, to reject those which were culturally and religiously "indigestible," and to adapt – that is, to Islamize - still others before adopting them. This process must, of course, be carried on in the present day and into the future. To rule it out would be to kill the culture and the religion.

A society's proper reaction to change implies two prerequisites. First, it needs a study and awareness of the total societal complex, each of whose institutions and factors is integrally interwoven with and dependent upon the others. Any suggestion for change regarding marriage practices, therefore, should not be investigated in isolation. It should be studied in relation to the other factors of individual and group welfare which those factors may affect. It might be argued, for instance, that, because of increased participation of women in the work force in many Muslim countries, the Islamic custom of mandatory male support for women should be abolished. Yet such a shortsighted view fails to take into account anything but the material aspects of the question. It might be counter-argued that much more important in this Islamic stipulation is the reinforcement it gives to the interdependence of the marriage partners; to break those bonds of rights for women and obligations for men would cut deeply into the strength of the marriage bond.

Similarly, some contemporaries might argue that Islam is old-fashioned in its unshakable condemnation of sex outside of marriage. They would cite contraceptive devices and new attitudes toward the sexual freedom of women as demanding a reappraisal of an old Islamic "fixation." But Islam's reason for rejecting greater sexual freedom was not that no adequate contraceptives were available in earlier times to prevent children born out of wedlock, nor did it insist on the importance of female virginity in order to discriminate against women or set a "double standard." Rather, Islam promoted this idea in order to strengthen the institutions of marriage and the family by making them carry benefits that could not be achieved elsewhere. To destroy the uniqueness of such marital benefits in an attempt to provide complete sexual equity would carry widespread and debilitating effects, not only for those institutions, but equally for the individuals who make up those institutions. We do not have to surmise about the effect on women that this innovation might have, for a living example is available in Western society. The consequences are already glaringly apparent. The increased sexual dispensability of the wife which this new promiscuity produces is one of the factors leading to the increased divorce rate. It also has drastically adverse effects on both the financial and emotional security of middle-aged and older women. Proper reaction of a society to change, therefore, demands a careful screening of the elements of change and their results for compatibility with the rest of the culture's goals and institutions.

Second, in order for Muslims to avoid rash acceptance of drastic and harmful changes in their marriage laws and customs, they must purge their society of the misuse of existent laws and customs. Often it is the widespread neglect or circumvention of the Qur'ānic or legal prescriptives which are at the root of the problem, rather than the institutions and practices themselves. A case in point is the misuse of the institution of *talāq*, many instances of which fail to comply with the regulations and restrictions which have been established for it. Adherence to those regulations and restrictions would obviate the need for drastic changes in the institution.

The imbalances caused by rapid social change are probably inevitable factors in any society. At this period of history, they are particularly challenging. Without careful reappraisal of the side-effects of contemplated innovation and its compatibility with other aspects of the religion and culture, and without a purging of misapplications of extant institutions, massive social disorientation and deleterious effects on the members of any society are inevitable. This is the contemporary challenge, not only for Muslim society, but also for every other society in the world.

Notes

1. In Christianity, marriage was first recognized as a sacrament in the twelfth century, when Peter Lombard's "Sentences" (Book 4, dist. 1, num. 2) enumerated marriage as one of the seven sacraments. That work became the standard textbook of Catholic theology during the Middle Ages and was formally accepted by the Councils of Florence (1439) and Trent (1545-1563).
2. Muhammad ibn Isma'īl al Bukhāri, *Sahih Al-Bukhāri*, tr. Muhammad Muhsin Khān. Al-Medinal al-Munauwara: Islamic University, 1974. Vol. 7, pp. 2-5, 8.

3. To this day, in the highly Westernized society of Beirut, Lebanon, unmarried young people are often embarrassed by the constant social pressures on them to marry.

4. The Qur'ān is the word of God dictated verbatim to the Prophet Muhammad. Its basic ethical principles and prescriptive laws, therefore, carry the authenticity of divine provenance. These principles and laws are designated as the *sharī'ah* ("path"). The human elaboration and interpretation of the *sharī'ah*, i.e., its development into specific laws by the jurists of the five schools of law (four Sunnī and one Shī'ī *madhāhib*, s. madhhab), is the subject matter of Islamic jurisprudence or *fiqh*.

5. Hammūdah 'Abd al 'Atī, *The Family Structure in Islam* (Indianapolis: American Trust Publications, 1977), p. 50.

6. The Qur'ān and Islamic law, reflecting the practice of slavery which existed in the pre and early Islamic periods, also condoned cohabitation of a master with his slave girls (Qur'ān 23:5-7; 70:29-31). Although most Muslims would try to rationalize the existence of the passages sanctioning this form of extramarital sex (see 'Abd al 'Atī, *Family Structures*, pp. 41-49) and draw attention to the companion mechanisms which legitimized the children of such unions, enjoined emancipation for the mothers, and generally controlled and regulated the practice, few, if any, Muslims today would regard sex as legitimate except within the bonds of marriage.

7. The Qur'ān contains not only repeated references to the rights of kin (17:23; 4:7-9; 8:41; etc.) but also inheritance and support provisions which are stipulated as reaching far beyond the nuclear family (2:180-182; 4:33, 176; etc.). Dire punishment is threatened for those who ignore these measures for intra-family support (4:7-12).

   While the commune dwellers in the 1960's in America realized rightly the benefits to their children of a family environment larger than that of the nuclear family, their experiments often resulted in frustration because of the weakness or nonexistence of a strong marriage bond between the procreative or adoptive parents. For various reasons, there were considerable instability and mobility among the adult members of the communes. Children, therefore, were constantly faced with the problems of separation from those parents whom they had come to know and love and of rebuilding substitute "parental" relationships with new arrivals to the group. This brought psychological problems for all members of the group, but especially for the children.

8. Exogamy is the custom of marrying only outside one's own tribe, clan, or family, i.e., outbreeding; endogamy is the opposite, i.e., inbreeding.

9. Prohibited to you (for marriage) are: Your mothers, daughters, sisters; father's sisters, mother's sisters; brother's daughters, sister's daughters; foster-mothers; (who gave you suck), foster-sisters; your wives' mothers; your step-daughters under your guardianship, born of your wives to whom you have gone in, no prohibition if you have not gone in; (those who have been) wives of your sons proceeding from your loins; and two sisters in wedlock at one and the same time, except for what is past; for God is Oft-forgiving Most Merciful. (Qur'ān 4:23) See also al Bukhārī, *Sahīh Al-Bukhārī*, pp. 28-34.

10 The Qur'ānic passage stating that it is unlawful for men to marry their "milk relatives" is to be found in 4:23. See note 9 above and al Bukhārī, *Sahīh Al-Bukhārī*, pp. 24-28.

11 'Abd al 'Atī, *Family Structure*, p. 131; al Bukhārī, *Sahīh Al-Bukhārī*, pp. 28-34.

12 The ever-widening problems of impotence in contemporary males may in large

part be a result of the excessive sexual freedom and familiarity which pertains in many of the societies of this century. see G.L. Ginsberg, et al., "The New Impotency," *Archives of General Psychology* 28 (1972): 218; and G.F. Gilder, *Sexual Suicide* (New York: Quadrangle/The New York Times Book Co., 1973).

13   See 'Abd al 'Atī, *Family Structure*, p. 139.

14   In Turkey and Pakistan, men and women can marry at eighteen and sixteen years of age, respectively; in Egypt, at nineteen and seventeen; in Jordan, at eighteen and seventeen; in Morocco and Iran, at eighteen and fifteen; and in Tunisia, at twenty for both sexes. Marriage of younger persons must have the consent of guardians and the permission of the court.

15   For example, barrenness of the first wife, disbalance of male/female population, chronic illness of the wife, large numbers of helpless widows and orphans in the community, and so forth.

16   See Tanzil-ur-Rahman, *A Code of Muslim Personal Law* (Karachi: Hamdard Academy, 1978), pp. 94-101, for a summary of modern legislation pertaining to polygyny. The Tunisian Law of 1956 [enacted by a secular government] prohibits it outright, while other countries have placed various restrictions on having more than one wife – e.g., financial ability of the husband, just cause, consent of the first wife or wives, and/or permission of a court or *ad hoc* council.

17.   Al Bukhārī, *Sahīh Al-Bukhārī*, pp. 51-53.

18.   Tanzil-ur-Rahman, *Code, pp. 51-52.*

19.   *'Abd al 'Atī, Family Structure*, pp. 76-84. Tanzil-ur-Rahman, *Code*, chap. 3, see especially pp. 71-74, for modern legislation in various Muslim countries relating to consent to marriage.

20.   Al Bukhārī, *Sahīh Al-Bukhārī*, pp. 51, 55, 59-61.

21.   Asaf A. A. Fyzee, *Outlines of Muhammadan Law*, 2nd ed. (London: Oxford University Press, 1955), pp. 112-113; Tanzil-ur-Rahman, *Code*, pp. 218-221.

22.   This paraphrases a *hadīth* from the life of the Prophet Muhammad: "Of all the permitted acts the one disliked most by God is divorce" (S. Ameenul Hasan Rizvi, "Women and Marriage in Islam," *The Muslim World League Journal*, vol. 12, no. 1 (Muharram, 1404 A.H. [October, 1984], p. 26).

23.   Tanzil-ur-Rahman, *Code*, pp. 313-316; Fyzee, *Outlines*, pp. 128-130.

24.   Fyzee, *Outlines*, pp. 130-131.

25.   Tanzil-ur-Rahman, *Code*, chap. 12, pp. 339 ff.; Fyzee, *Outlines*, pp. 134-135.

26.   Tanzil-ur-Rahman, *Code*, pp. 346-350.

27.   Ibid., pp. 552ff.; Fyzee, *Outlines*, pp. 138-139; Alhaji A. D. Ajijola, *Introduction to Islamic Law* (Karachi: International Islamic Publishers for Ajijola Memorial Islamic Publishing Co. (Nigeria], 1981), pp. 172ff.

28.   Tanzil-ur-Rahman, *Code,* pp. 504ff.; Ajijola, *Introduction*, pp. 176-177; Fyzee, *Outlines*, pp. 141-142.